CALEDONIAN
STEAM PACKET COMPANY LTD

Duchess of Hamilton about to depart from Gourock on a Clyde River Steamer Club charter to Arrochar.

CALEDONIAN
STEAM PACKET COMPANY LTD

Alistair Deayton

TEMPUS

Acknowledgements

The illustrations in this book have come from many sources, most collected by myself over the past thirty years or so. Many are from postcard-size photographs produced for sale by the Clyde River Steamer Club. Most of those from the mid-sixties onwards are from colour slides taken by myself.

The main source of information has been what is *the* book on the subject of Clyde Steamers: *Clyde River and Other Steamers* by C.L.D. Duckworth and G.E. Langmuir. Also helpful have been *Classic Scottish Paddle Steamers* by Alan Paterson, and a number of back issues of the CRSC annual magazine *Clyde Steamers* and from articles from some of their booklets produced for special cruises.

Information about the two Railway Steamboat Companies has come from a series of articles in *The True Line*, the magazine of the Caledonian Railway Association.

My thanks to: Ian McCrorie and George Owen for further information on the 1852 steamers; CRSC Archivist Archie McCallum for access to old handbills and some photographs; Bruce Peter for the loan of a couple of photographs taken by his grandfather, A. Ernest Glen; the staff of the Glasgow Room, Mitchell Library for access to the Wotherspoon and Langmuir collections; Admeto Verde and Antonio Scrimali for information and photographs of Clyde Steamers that ended up in Italy and Greece; Richard Orr for a view of the ex-*Marchioness of Graham*; Robin Boyd; Iain Quinn and Andrew Clark for use of photographs; Iain Quinn also for checking over the text for factual errors and for going over the final proofs.

First published 2002
Copyright © Alistair Deayton, 2002

Tempus Publishing Limited
The Mill, Brimscombe Port,
Stroud, Gloucestershire, GL5 2QG

ISBN 0 7524 2381 9

TYPESETTING AND ORIGINATION BY
Tempus Publishing Limited
PRINTED IN GREAT BRITAIN BY
Midway Colour Print, Wiltshire

The funnel of *Duchess of Hamilton* in September 1970 during her final period in service.

Contents

Acknowledgements   4

Introduction   7

1.   Before the CSP: 1842-1868   10

2.   Caledonian Railway-Owned: 1889-1922   20

3.   LMS-Owned: 1923-1947   70

4.   Nationalised: 1948-1972   123

Vignette of *Galatea* (from a CSP envelope). (*CRSC Archive*).

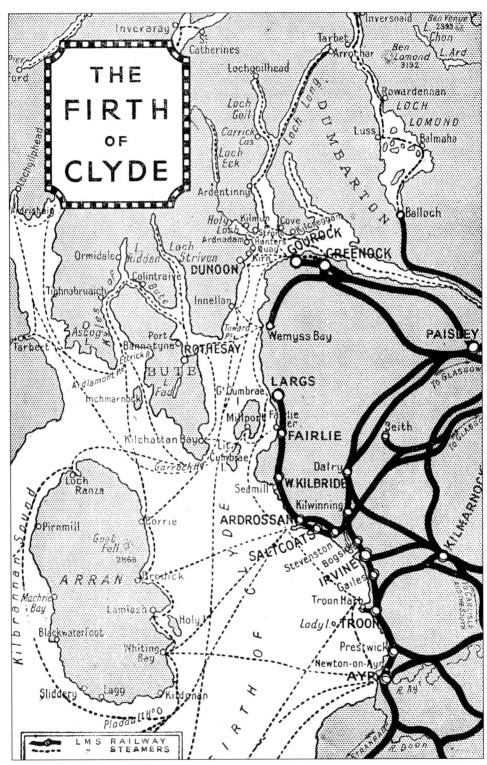

A map from the 1935 summer timetable.

Introduction

The Caledonian Steam Packet Co. Ltd was formed in 1889 as the steamer-owning arm of the Caledonian Railway, when the railway extended from Greenock to Gourock. It continued as an entity after the great railway grouping of 1923 when it became part of the London Midland & Scottish Railway, and after the Nationalization of 1948, when it came under control of the Railway Executive. From 1953 it was controlled by the British Transport Commission and, from 1964, the British Railways Board. In 1969 it became part of the Scottish Transport Group, along with David MacBrayne Ltd and the Scottish Bus Group, and on 1 January 1973 was merged with MacBrayne to form Caledonian MacBrayne. At the great railway merger of 1923 the CSP absorbed the GSWR steamers and services from Greenock Princes Pier, Fairlie and Ardrossan Winton Pier. In 1936 the steamers of Williamson-Buchanan and Turbine Steamers - apart from *Queen Alexandra* and *King George V* - were taken over, and on 1 January 1948, the LNER steamers and their services from Craigendoran became part of the CSP fleet. These companies' steamers, including their time under the CSP flag, are dealt with in other books in this series, and hence are not included in this volume.

In 1841, the Glasgow, Paisley & Greenock Railway opened to Greenock, Cathcart Street. Initially the privately owned steamer operators were reluctant to provide connecting services, but in 1842 the Railway Steamboat Company was formed to operate rail-connected steamer services and purchased three steamers; *Isle of Bute*, *Maid of Bute*, and *Royal Victoria*. In 1844 three new steamers were built for the Railway Steamboat Co., *Pilot*, *Petrel*, and *Pioneer*. The latter two had long and notable careers after leaving the ownership of the Railway Steamboat Co. At the end of 1846 this first attempt at railway ownership of steamers ceased and the fleet was sold. In August 1851 the Caledonian Railway took over the Glasgow, Paisley, & Greenock Railway, and in 1852 tried again with a new Railway Steamboat Co. Two new steamers, *Helensburgh* and *Dunoon* were built but only lasted one season in service. The smaller newly-built *Gourock* was purchased later in the season, but only lasted a few months in service. Although advertised and reported in contemporary newspapers, this trio seem to have escaped the attention of steamer historians including Williamson, McQueen, Duckworth and Langmuir, and others. The next year *Glasgow Citizen*, *Eva*, and the eight-year-old *Loch Lomond* were used by the company, along with *Flamingo*. At the end of the 1853 season the Railway Steamboat Co. wound up operations and a deal was reached with the private owners for rail-connected services from Greenock.

In 1865 the Wemyss Bay Railway Company reached Wemyss Bay from Port Glasgow. The railway-owned Wemyss Bay Steampacket Company had been formed the previous year in preparation for this event. Two large saloon steamers were ordered from Caird of Greenock in early 1864. The first of these was sold for blockade running in the American Civil War, and a replacement was ordered. These two were joined by the smaller *Largs*, which had come from the yard of Wingate at Port Glasgow, and had been completed in autumn 1864. In April 1865, before the railway was completed, *Largs* started running from Glasgow to Millport, extending to Arran from early May. On 15 May the railway opened and *Kyles*, the first of the Caird twins, entered service from Wemyss Bay to Tighnabruaich, joined by *Largs* sailing to Brodick. A flush-decked steamer named *Victory* was purchased at the end of May and *Bute*, the second Caird-built steamer, entered service at the end of June. *Kyles* was put on excursion service from Wemyss Bay, and later in 1865 both *Kyles* and *Bute* commenced sailing from Glasgow. In 1866 both *Kyles* and *Bute* were sold to the Thames, the former becoming *Albert Edward*, and the latter gaining notoriety as *Princess Alice* when she sank in 1878 after a collision on the river with the loss of around 800 lives. The almost new *Argyle* was purchased to replace them on the Wemyss Bay services, which continued for the next three seasons. At the end of 1868, the Wemyss Bay Steamboat Co. ceased operations, and from 1870 Gillies & Campbell, who purchased *Largs* and *Argyle*, maintained the rail-connected services from Wemyss Bay.

On 1 June 1889, the railway's extension from Greenock Cathcart Street, now Greenock Central, to Gourock was opened and the Caledonian Steam Packet Co. Ltd commenced operations, under the able leadership of Captain James Williamson. At the end of the previous year *Meg Merrilies* and *Madge Wildfire* had been purchased from Peter and Alex Campbell of Kilmun, who were moving to the Bristol Channel. They received the distinctive pre-1914 CSP colours of navy blue hull, with white boot topping and two gold lines round the hull, white paddle boxes and deck saloons, with pink railings and panels on the sponsons and a yellow funnel right to the top. What a pity that these colours vanished before colour photography. Two new steamers were ordered for the 1889 season, *Caledonia* and *Galatea*, the latter a large two-funnelled steamer with two-crank compound machinery, whereas *Caledonia* had a tandem compound. Captain Williamson's own command, the teetotal steamer *Ivanhoe* also entered rail-connected service.

Three new steamers entered service in 1890, notable in that on each the bridge was forward of the funnel. *Marchioness of Breadalbane* and *Marchioness of Bute* were near sisters, while *Duchess of Hamilton* was a larger and faster steamer for the Ardrossan to Brodick run. A third Marchioness, *Marchioness of Lorne*, the same length as the other two but two feet beamier entered service in 1891. She was designed as a winter Arran steamer.

In 1895 *Duchess of Rothesay* was built, to compete with the GSWR's *Mercury*, and in 1897 *Ivanhoe* was purchased by the CSP. Her paddle boxes were painted white and she ceased being teetotal when a bar was added. 1902 saw the advent of *Duchess of Montrose*, which replaced *Meg Merrilies*, and 1903 saw the building of *Duchess of Fife*, a steamer that was to remain in service for half a century. Also in 1903, a new station was opened at Wemyss Bay and a large and magnificent pier opened, most of which survives to the present day.

In 1901 the pioneer turbine, *King Edward*, had appeared on the Clyde, followed a year later by the first *Queen Alexandra*. In 1906 the CSP took delivery of its first turbine steamer, *Duchess of Argyll*, intended to beat the GSWR's *Glen Sannox* on the Arran route.

In 1908 the Caledonian and GSW Railways commenced a period of co-operation to eliminate the wasteful competition on the major routes, e.g. from Greenock and Gourock to Rothesay and from Ardrossan to Arran. This enabled *Marchioness of Bute* to be sold in 1908 and *Ivanhoe* and *Madge Wildfire* in 1911.

The First World War saw the requisitioning of the entire fleet by the Admiralty, and a number of steamers had to be chartered to cover the essential services, notably *Iona* and *Fusilier* from MacBrayne's, and *Benmore* and *Ivanhoe* from Captain John Williamson. *Duchess of Hamilton* was sunk by a mine while in service as a minesweeper in November 1915, *Duchess of Montrose* was sunk off Dunkirk in March 1917 and *Marchioness of Lorne* did not re-enter service after war duty, eventually being scrapped in 1923. After the war the blue hulls were replaced by black ones.

1923 saw the great railway amalgamation and the formation of the 'Big Four' railway companies. The Caledonian and GSWR were absorbed into the London Midland & Scottish Railway, and the GSWR steamers were absorbed into the CSP fleet, although technically owned by the LMSR. A combined colour scheme was tried for 1923 and 1924 with the so-called 'tartan lum', yellow with a red band and black top. In 1925 the buff black-topped funnel was introduced and which continued until the formation of Caledonian MacBrayne in 1973.

After the 1924 season the Arran paddle steamer *Glen Sannox* needed reboilering, and it was decided to scrap her and replace her by a turbine steamer. A repeat of *Duchess of Argyll* was ordered and named *Glen Sannox*, entering service in May 1925.

The 1930s saw a plethora of steamers being built for the CSP, commencing in 1930 with the turbine *Duchess of Montrose*. This was a great advance on previous steamers, with an enclosed promenade deck and a deck saloon forward in that area. She was placed on excursion duty, and was followed two years later by *Duchess of Hamilton*, a repeat of the same design, which was placed on the Ayr excursion service. 1934 saw the introduction of two new paddle steamers *Caledonia* and *Mercury*, notable for their concealed paddle box design. The former was to survive until 1969 and be the penultimate Clyde paddle steamer in service. A smaller version of this duo, *Marchioness of Lorne*, appeared in 1935 for the Holy Loch route. 1935 also saw the first motor vessel in the fleet, *Wee Cumbrae*, designed for the Largs to Millport run.

In October 1935 the five ships of Williamson-Buchanan Steamers were purchased, and in 1936 the turbine *Marchioness of Graham*, similar in size to *Caledonia* and *Mercury*, was built for the Arran service, as was the puffer-like motor cargo ship *Arran Mail*, for the early morning mail run to Arran.

The CSP's last paddle steamers, and indeed last steamers, *Juno* and *Jupiter*, entered service in 1937, and the following year saw the appearance of *Ashton* and *Leven*, two small motor vessels, utilized for sightseeing cruises on the Clyde during the Empire Exhibition of that year, and which were later to serve the Largs to Millport run.

The 1939-1945 war saw the majority of the fleet called up for active service, with two losses, *Mercury*, which was sunk while minesweeping in December 1940 and *Juno* in March 1941 by a bomb which dropped on her while berthed in London Docks. *Duchess of Rothesay*, while surviving the war, was considered too worn-out in 1946 to be reconditioned for civilian service and was scrapped.

Railway nationalization saw the LNER steamers become part of the fleet on 1 January 1948.

In 1952 the small motor vessel *Countess of Breadalbane*, which had been sailing on Loch Awe, was brought overland to Inveraray and entered service on the Clyde.

The need for car ferry services had been recognized as far back as 1939, when plans were drawn up for a steam lift-loading car ferry, and in 1953-1954 the first car ferries were built. To avoid the necessity of constructing link spans at the various terminals, a unique system of hoist-loading was utilized, with turntables on the hoist and forward on the car deck to enable cars to turn. *Arran, Bute* and *Cowal* were designed to cover the expected services to these areas, and routes were established from Gourock to Dunoon, Wemyss Bay to Rothesay and Ardrossan, and Fairlie to Brodick with thrice weekly cargo runs from Wemyss Bay to Millport. Four mid-size motor vessels, *Maid of Argyll*, *Maid of Ashton*, *Maid of Cumbrae*, and *Maid of Skelmorlie* also arrived at this time, introducing such delights as forenoon café cruises and afternoon cruises to such destinations as Dunagoil Bay, as well as serving the Holy Loch, and enabling the veteran *Duchess of Fife* to be withdrawn. The ABC car ferries were really too small for the Arran run, and a larger version, *Glen Sannox*, entered service there in 1957.

In 1961 *Jupiter* was sold for scrapping. The *Duchess of Montrose* and *Jeanie Deans* were withdrawn in 1964 with cutbacks in the excursion programme, including the entire programme from Ayr, apart from a Friday cruise by *Duchess of Hamilton*, with the moving of *Caledonia* to Craigendoran. In 1965 the remaining vessels adopted a variation of British Rail's (as it had then become) new Corporate Identity, with Monastral Blue hulls. Fortunately the Clyde was spared the red funnel with the double arrow symbol on it as on of the remainder of the railway fleet, but all the vessels received red lions on the funnels.

In 1967 the Tilbury ferry *Rose* was transferred to the CSP and renamed *Keppel* for the Largs to Millport service.

On 1 January 1969, the CSP was taken out of Railway control, and became part of the Scottish Transport Group.

After the 1969 season, *Caledonia* was withdrawn. A Swedish roll-on roll-off car ferry, *Stena Baltica*, was purchased for the Arran service, for which link spans were now provided, and renamed *Caledonia*. *Glen Sannox* was converted to stern-loading at the same time.

In 1972 new car ferry services were introduced from Largs to Cumbrae Slip and from Lochranza to Claonaig in Kintyre, and *Kilbrannan*, the first of a new class of landing-craft type car ferries, mainly for West Highland routes, was introduced on the Lochranza to Claonaig route. 1972 also saw the closure of Craigendoran and Arrochar piers.

1 January 1973 saw the formation of Caledonian MacBrayne, the integration of the Western Isles and Clyde fleets, and the adoption of the red black-topped funnel with yellow circle and lion. But that, as they say, is another story, and is not yet the preserve of a historical volume such as this.

One

Before the CSP
1842-1868

Maid of Bute, above, along with her sister *Isle of Bute*, were both built in 1835 by John Wood at Port Glasgow for the Rothesay to Glasgow service. In 1841 they were chartered by the Glasgow, Paisley & Greenock Railway, along with *Flambeau* (1840), to run from Greenock to Dunoon and Rothesay. *Victor* (1836) and *Warrior* (1839) served Largs while *Vale of Leven* (1836) and *Maid of Leven* (1839) ran to Helensburgh, Roseneath and Row (as Rhu was then spelt). *Lochgoil* (1841) ran to Inveraray and *Royal Victoria* (1838) and *Superb* (1839) were used in the early part of the season. All these were wooden-hulled except *Flambeau*, *Maid of Leven* and *Royal Victoria*, which were iron-hulled. At the beginning of 1842 the railway company formed the Railway Steam Packet Co. to operate steamers, and purchased *Maid of Bute* and *Isle of Bute*. *Royal Victoria* also ran for them to Helensburgh and the Gareloch in 1842 and 1843. Barr & MacNab in Paisley had built her. They were not originally located near the river and her hull had been hauled through Paisley by a team of heavy horses to a field beside the River Cart, where she was launched sideways. She was sold back to her builders in 1845, continuing to operate on the same service. In 1846 she was sold to the Dundee & Perth Steam Packet Company and later to Preston owners. No record of the subsequent history of *Maid of Bute* and *Isle of Bute* exists. (*G.E. Langmuir Collection, Mitchell Library*)

In 1844, *Pilot* and *Pioneer* were built for the Railway Steam Packet Co. by Barr & MacNab who had, by this time, established a riverside shipyard. *Pioneer* is seen here at Ballachulish Quarries c.1859 in her original condition. No illustration of *Pilot* has survived. The company sold her to G&J Burns in February 1847, along with the remainder of its steamers. She saw service in the next three years on their Clyde and West Highland routes. In 1850 she was operated on Loch Lomond by G&J Burns and on 19 July of that year hit a rock near Rowardennan, which has since been known as the Pilot Rock. *Waterwitch*, the other steamer on the loch, took on board the passengers and a month later *Pilot* was salvaged and towed to Balloch for repairs. She continued sailing on the loch until October of that year. In 1851 she was sold to Captain Gillies of the Wemyss Bay Steamboat Co., and in 1855 to Belfast owners for the Belfast to Bangor service, which she operated until scrapped in 1862.

Pioneer, seen here at Oban post-1874, was a more attractive vessel, with a reputation for speed. After sale to G&J Burns, she continued on the Greenock to Rothesay route, but operated from around 1848 on the Glasgow to Ardrishaig route, and was transferred to David Hutcheson & Co. with the remainder of Burns' West Highland fleet in 1852. Replaced by *Mountaineer* in 1852, she moved to Oban. In 1862 she went ashore at Greenock and broke her back. It is probable that in the repairs after this incident she received her clipper bow. In the winter of 1874-1875 she was lengthened, a slanting stem replaced the clipper bow, deck salons were fitted, she was re-boilered and a second funnel added. She was withdrawn at the end of the 1893 summer season and was sold for scrap in 1895. *(G.E. Langmuir Collection, Mitchell Library)*

Petrel followed from Barr & MacNab in 1845. She differed in having two funnels, and operated from Greenock to Largs and Millport. She was a notably fast steamer for her time. In 1855 she ran on the Lochgoilhead route for a time. In 1858 she was sold for use as a Sunday-breaker. At that time pubs in Scotland were forbidden by law from opening on Sundays and Sunday travel was frowned on by douce Presbyterian Scotland. A Sunday cruise down the Clyde was seen as an excuse by many to get blind drunk, and the term Sunday-breaker became notorious in Clyde Steamer history. (*Wotherspoon Collection, Mitchell Library*)

From 1860 to 1864, *Petrel* was chartered to run in opposition to *Pilot* from Belfast to Bangor. In 1865, after many of her competitors were sold to run the blockade in the US Civil War, she was rebuilt with a single funnel and is seen here at the Broomielaw in a George Washington Wilson photograph, probably in 1867. She was later used on the Largs to Arran route and was broken up in 1885. Behind her is *Rothesay Castle* (1865).

In 1852 the Caledonian Railway revived the Railway Steamboat Co. Some seven steamers were used in that year, but *Loch Lomond* is the only one for which an illustration is available.

Helensburgh was launched at the yard of Laurence Hill & Co. of Port Glasgow on 10 May 1852 for the Railway Steamboat Co. Her machinery was built by Scott, Sinclair & Co. She ran a VIP cruise on 29 May to the Holy Loch and entered service on 1 June from Greenock to Helensburgh and piers to Garelochead. This steamer and *Dunoon* were noted for a lack of speed and both were sold after the 1852 season. Both were sold to an Australian owner and *Helensburgh* was renamed *Melbourne*. Gold had been discovered at Ballarat and Bendigo in 1851 and these were Australian gold rush years. She went out to Melbourne under sail, arriving there in March 1853. Initially used in the trade to Geelong, she was purchased in August 1854 by Captain Francis Cadell, pioneer of navigation on the Murray River. She sailed through the Murray mouth on 19 August for the goldfields of Beechwood and Ovena with cargo. She retuned to the sea on 28 August, and later ran from Adelaide to Goolwa until wrecked while entering the Murray Mouth on 16 November 1859.

Dunoon, a sister of *Helensburgh*, and was launched on 7 June 1852 from the same yard and was probably in service by the end of that month. She was advertised to sail to Dunoon and the Holy Loch. She was sold to Australian owners, renamed *Geelong*, and left Greenock under sail on 4 November 1852. On 18 November she sank in the Bay of Biscay.

Gourock was built in 1852 by Scotts at Cartsdyke, engined by Scott, Sinclair & Co. and was 22ft shorter than her two fleetmates. She had initially been part owned by Thomas Seath, who was also her master. Four of the other six shareholders were Glaswegian wine and spirit merchants. She was advertised from 5 April 1852, to sail from Glasgow Bridge to Greenock and Gourock. In August 1852 she was sold to a group of owners, who were nominees for the Caledonian Railway, and, in April 1853, it was recorded that she was 'sold to foreigners'.

Glasgow Citizen was a larger vessel used in the 1853 season. She had been built the previous year by J. Barr who had operated her from Glasgow to Rothesay in that season, and she operated from

EXPEDITIOUS AND FREQUENT COMMUNICATION
BETWEEN
GLASGOW, PAISLEY, GREENOCK, AND THE COAST,
PER CALEDONIAN RAILWAY & STEAMERS.

| HELENSBURGH, | — | — | — | Capt. M'PHERSON. |
| DUNOON, | — | — | — | Capt. SHIELDS. |

ON TUESDAY, 1st June, and till further Notice, the TRAINS and Steamer "HELENSBURGH" are intended to Depart from the various Stations as follows, or as soon thereafter as circumstances will permit.

Time taken from the Railway Clocks.

HELENSBURGH, ROW, ROSENEATH, SHANDON, AND GARELOCH-HEAD.

DOWN TRAINS AND STEAMERS.

TRAINS LEAVE	A.M.	A.M.	P.M.	P.M.	P.M.
Glasgow, ——— at	8 0	10 0	2 0	4 0	6 0
Paisley, ——— ,,	8 15	10 15	2 15	4 14	6 15
STEAMERS LEAVE GREENOCK on Arrival of Trains, for					
Helensburgh, Row, Roseneath, ——— about	9 0	11 0	3 0	4 50	7 0
Shandon, ——— ,,		11 0		4 50	7 0
Rahane, Gareloch-head ,,		11 0			7 0

UP STEAMERS AND TRAINS.

STEAMERS LEAVE	A.M.	A.M.	P.M.	P.M.	
Gareloch-head, ——— about	7 30		1 0		
Rahane, ——— ,,	7 40		1 10		
Shandon, ——— ,,	7 45		1 20		5 55
Roseneath, ——— ,,	7 55	9 30	1 30	3 30	6 5
Row, ——— ,,	8 0	9 35	1 35	3 35	6 10
Helensburgh, ——— ,,	8 15	9 50	1 50	3 50	6 25
TRAINS LEAVE GREENOCK on Arrival of Steamers, for					
Glasgow, ——— ,,	8 45	10 30	2 30	4 30	7 15
Paisley, ——— ,,	9 15	10 30	2 30	4 30	7 15

The 8.45 A.M. Up Train and the 4 P.M. Down Train being Express, are expected to make the run to and from Greenock and Glasgow in 45 minutes.

The Railway and Steamboat Companies do not hold themselves responsible for any irregularities that may take place connected with the above-named Hours, either as regards the Railway or Steamers.

PASSENGERS ARE BOOKED CONDITIONALLY, that is in case only there be room in the Train or Steamers for which they are booked; and they are requested to look after their own Luggage, the Companies not being in any way responsible for it.

THROUGH TICKETS SOLD AT THE RAILWAY STATIONS AND ON BOARD THE STEAMERS.

RETURN TICKETS issued daily. Those issued on Saturdays are available on Mondays.

FARES.

TO OR FROM GLASGOW AND ANY OF ABOVE PLACES.	SINGLE TICKET.	RETURN TICKET.
1st Class of Railway and Cabin of Steamer,	2s 9d	4s 6d
2d Class of Railway and Cabin of Steamer,	1s 9d	3s
3d Class of Railway & Steerage of Steamer,	1s 2d	2s

TO OR FROM PAISLEY AND ANY OF ABOVE PLACES.	SINGLE TICKET.	RETURN TICKET.
1st Class of Railway and Cabin of Steamer,	2s 3d	3s 9d
2d Class of Railway and Cabin of Steamer,	1s 7d	2s 9d
3d Class of Railway & Steerage of Steamer,	1s	1s 9d

TIME TICKETS per Railway and Steamers, at Reduced Rates, for periods of One Month and upwards, may be had on application at the Railway Stations.

FARES from Greenock and back per Steamers, Cabin, 1s.; Steerage, 8d. Children under fourteen years of age, Half-fare; under ten years of age, Free.

The Dunoon, Kirn, Strone, and Kilmun Steamer will be on the station in about a fortnight. The Hours of Sailing will be given in future Advertisements.

Greenock, May, 1853.

Greenock to Innellan and Rothesay in 1853. She sailed for Australia in late December 1853 at the same time as a clipper. The master of the clipper told the master of the *Citizen* that he would inform the harbour authorities at Melbourne that *Glasgow Citizen* was on her way. However the ex-steamer was a very fast ship, making at least 12 knots under sail and reached Melbourne some fourteen days prior to the clipper. By the time the clipper arrived, *Glasgow Citizen* had had her engine and paddles refitted and was in steam on the Melbourne to Geelong service. She sailed on 15 October 1862 for Dunedin, New Zealand, with a large passenger list of gold diggers, but was never heard of again.

Eva was newly built in 1853 by Denny of Dumbarton and served the Gareloch service. She was also sold to Australia and left under sail on 27 December 1853. Her paddles and engines had been removed and a mast fitted in place of her funnel. She sank in a storm shortly after leaving the Clyde. Six of the crew survived, but the captain, his wife, sister-in-law and seven other crew members perished.

The Railway Steam Packet Co. used a fourth steamer, named *Flamingo*, in the 1853 season. She had been built in that year at the yard of James Ward Hoby at East Renfrew. In November of that year she was registered as *Bellbird* and sailed for Port Philip Bay. She was sighted on 22 December some 360 miles west-south-west of Madeira, but nothing more was heard of her and she was lost with all hands somewhere in the middle of the Atlantic.

Loch Lomond had been built in 1845 by Denny of Dumbarton, their first steamer, and engined by Smith & Rodger. She had a forerunner of the engine room telegraph fitted. In 1853 she was used by the Railway Steam Packet Co. and probably operated on the shorter routes from Greenock. In 1854 she was sold for use on the Mersey on the Eastham ferry service, and in 1862 she was sold to Preston owners where she was broken up two years later.

Opposite below: The Wemyss Bay Steam Packet Co. was formed early in 1864, prior to the completion of the railway to that pier. Two large saloon paddle steamers were ordered from Caird & Co. of Greenock. The first was launched on 17 August 1864, but had already been sold for blockade running and left for the Confederate States named *Hattie*. She was lost at sea on 8 May 1865. The second steamer to be ordered, *Kyles*, was launched on 15 October 1864 and was in service by 15 May 1865 when the railway opened, operating from Wemyss Bay to Tighnabruiach. *Bute*, which had been ordered to replace *Hattie*, entered service at the beginning of June but both steamers were then transferred to run from the Broomielaw from 10 August, *Bute* to Arran via the Kyles and *Kyles* to Tighnabruiach. At the end of the season both *Kyles* and *Bute* were sold to the Thames, *Kyles* became *Albert Edward* and *Bute* became *Princess Alice*. *Kyles* was badly damaged en route to the Thames and had to put into Kingstown (now Dun Laoghaire) for repairs after storm damage. (*Peter Box Collection*)

Largs, seen to the left in this view of the original Wemyss Bay Pier, was built by T. Wingate & Co. of Port Glasgow, and was the first of the Wemyss Bay Co.'s steamers to be completed, in September 1864, some eight months prior to the completion of the railway. In April 1865 she started running from Broomielaw to Largs and Millport. At the beginning of May she extended this service to Arran, and from 15 May, when the railway was opened, operated from Wemyss Bay to Lamlash, spending the night at the latter pier. After the liquidation of the Wemyss Bay Steam Packet Co. in early 1869 she continued on railway-connected services from Wemyss Bay, under the ownership of her captain, James Gillies and his son-in-law Alexander Campbell. In 1877 she was sold to the Waterford SS Co., for whom she ran on the Shannon as *Mermaid* until 1903. Ahead of *Largs* in this illustration is *Lancelot* (1868), across the end of the pier is *Lady Gertrude* (1872), while *Argyle* is on the right hand side of the pier.

An advertisement for the Wemyss Bay Co. steamers dated 27 July 1865. Note that at this time, the times against the piers are not the arrival times at these piers, but the relevant departure time from Glasgow. (*G.E. Langmuir Collection, Mitchell Library*)

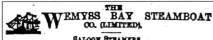

THE WEMYSS BAY STEAMBOAT CO. (LIMITED).

SALOON STEAMERS
"BUTE," "VICTORY," "KYLES," "LARGS."

ARRANGEMENTS,
Commencing 1st of AUGUST, 1865, till further Notice (*unless prevented by Weather or any unforeseen occurrence.*)

GLASGOW, ROTHESAY, KYLES OF BUTE, LARGS, FAIRLIE, MILLPORT, BRODICK, & LAMLASH (*Via WEMYSS BAY*).

Run in connection with the TRAINS on the WEMYSS BAY RAILWAY, as follows:—

DOWN.
Trains Leave BRIDGE STREET, *via* Wemyss Bay, for

	A.M.	A.M.	P.M.	P.M.	P.M.	P.M.	P.M.
BRODICK .... at	8 40	..	..	..	..	..	..
Colintraive	8 40	..	..	..	..	5 45	..
Fairlie	8 40	..	1 10	..	4 10	5 45	..
Innellan	8 40	..	2 10	2 30	4 10	5 45	..
Lamlash	8 40	..	..	..	..	..	..
Largs..........	8 40	..	1 10	..	4 10	5 45	..
Millport..........	8 40	..	1 10	..	4 10	5 45	..
Port-Bannatyne	..	..	..	..	..	5 45	..
ROTHESAY.....	8 40	10 10	1 10	2 30	4 10	5 45	..
Tighnabruich..	8 40	..	..	..	..	5 45	..
Toward..........	8 40	10 10	1 10	2 30	4 10	5 45	..

UP.
Steamers Returning to Wemyss Bay Railway for GLASGOW.

Leaving

	A.M.	A.M.	A.M.	P.M.	P.M.	P.M.	P.M.
BRODICK, about	..	..	..	..	2.30	..	..
Colintraive	6.15	..	..	..	..	..	..
Fairlie..........	..	7.50	..	11.5	4.25	..	..
Innellan,........	7.30	8.25	9.30	12.30	4.30	..	6.30
Lamlash	..	..	..	..	2.0	..	..
Largs	6.55	8.5	9.30	12.30	4.40	..	6.45
				A.M.			
Millport........	6.30	7.40	..	11.50	4.10	..	6.30
Port-Bannatyne	6.45	..	..	..	..	..	..
ROTHESAY.....	7.0	8.5	9.10	12.0	4.10	4.40	6.0
Tighnabruich..	5.50	..	..	..	..	..	..
Toward..........	7.12	8.12	9.23	12.12	4.22	..	6.12

Trains leave

Wemyss Bay at..	7.50	8.50	10.15	1.0	5.30	5.30	7.30
GLASGOW arrive	9.5	10.5	11 30	2.15	6.45	6.45	8.45

NOTE.—Passengers land free on Wemyss Bay Railway Wharf. All Steamers start by Railway time. Steamers start Ten Minutes earlier on Monday Mornings, for 7.50 and 8.50 A.M. Trains from Wemyss Bay.

BY ORDER.

Glasgow, August 1, 1865.

THE New Saloon Steamers "BUTE" and "KYLES" will RESUME GLASGOW SAILINGS on THURSDAY the 10th.

WEMYSS BAY STEAMBOAT CO. (LIMITED).

SPLENDID DAILY PLEASURE TRIP
TO
KYLES OF BUTE AND ARRAN.

On and after THURSDAY, 10th August, the New Saloon Steamer "BUTE" will sail every lawful day from GLASGOW at 7.30 A.M., calling at GREENOCK, KILCREGGAN, KIRN, DUNOON, and WEMYSS BAY (Train from Glasgow, 8 40 A.M.), and proceeding to INNELLAN, TOWARD, ROTHESAY, COLINTRAIVE, TIGHNABRUICH, BRODICK, and LAMLASH; Returning from LAMLASH about 2 P.M., calling at BRODICK, KILCHATTAN BAY, ROTHESAY, TOWARD, INNELLAN, WEMYSS BAY (Train from Wemyss Bay for Glasgow, 5.30 P.M.), and proceeding for DUNOON, KIRN, KILCREGGAN, and GREENOCK to GLASGOW.

Return Tickets issued on board.

July 27, 1865.

BY ORDER.

WEMYSS BAY STEAMBOAT CO. (LIMITED).

On and after THURSDAY, 10th Aug., until further Notice, the Splendid Saloon Steamer "KYLES" will Sail from GLASGOW at 4.10 P.M., direct for KILCREGGAN, KIRN, DUNOON, and WEMYSS BAY—Train from Glasgow, 5 45 P.M.—and proceeding for INNELLAN, TOWARD, ROTHESAY, PORT-BANNATYNE, COLINTRAIVE and TIGHNABRUICH; Returning following Morning, leaving TIGHNABRUICH at 5.50 A.M., for COLINTRAIVE, PORT-BANNATYNE, ROTHESAY, TOWARD, INNELLAN, and WEMYSS BAY—Train from Wemyss Bay to Glasgow, 7.50—and proceeding to DUNOON, KIRN, KILCREGGAN, direct for GLASGOW.

July 27, 1865.

BY ORDER.

WEMYSS BAY STEAMBOAT CO. (LIMITED).

This Company are prepared to Contract with Parties for PLEASURE EXCURSIONS, by Saloon Steamer "KYLES" or "BUTE."

Apply to Captain Rankin, Wemyss Bay.

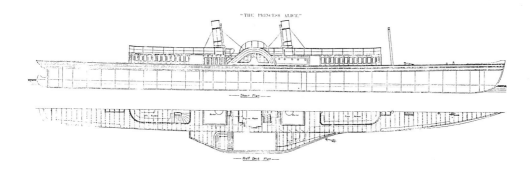

On 3 September 1878, *Princess Alice*, while returning from a day excursion to Sheerness, was run down one mile below Woolwich Arsenal by the collier *Bywell Castle*. She was almost cut in two and sank in five minutes. Of around 900 passengers and crew on board, only sixty-nine were saved, heralding the worst disaster in British pleasure steamer history.

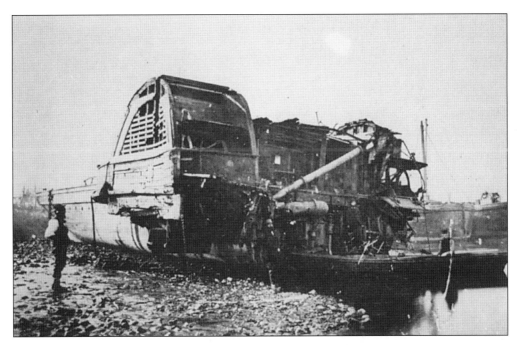

The paddle wheels and centre section of *Princess Alice* after she had been raised, showing where *Bywell Castle* had severed her hull. (*Peter Box Collection*)

17

The stern of *Princes Alice* after she was raised. It was said that the deck saloons were so crowded that some people died standing up and their bodies were found in that position. (*Peter Box Collection*)

Albert Edward continued on Thames service until 1888 when she was scrapped. She is seen here at Cannon Street Station.

At the end of May 1865, the Wemyss Bay Steam Packet Co. purchased *Victory* from Captain Duncan Stewart. Barclay Curle had built her in 1863 for his Glasgow to Rothesay service. She was taken over by Gillies & Campbell after the end of the Wemyss Bay SP Co., and was sold in 1871 to Duncan Dewar, who renamed her *Marquis of Lorne*, and used her as a Sunday-breaker. In 1882, on the opening of Fairlie Pier, she was purchased by Hill & Co. and again renamed *Cumbrae*. She remained on that service, probably till the GSWR took over the service in 1892, and ended her days as a coal hulk at Newry. (*G.E. Langmuir Collection, Mitchell Library*)

Argyle was also built by Barclay Curle for Captain Duncan Stewart, with machinery from *Alma* of 1855, which had been broken up in 1865. After only two weeks of service in 1866, she was sold to the Wemyss Bay SP Co., to replace *Kyles* and *Bute*. She went to Gillies & Campbell, and remained on Wemyss Bay railway connection services until 1890. She was sold for service on the Tay, where she is seen at Newburgh, until scrapped in 1909. (*David Edwards, A. Ernest Glen Collection*)

Two

Caledonian Railway-
Owned: 1889-1922

Meg Merrilies was one of the two steamers purchased from Peter & Alexander Campbell of Kilmun for the commencement of services from Gourock in 1889. Barclay Curle had built her in 1883 for the North British Steam Packet Co. Ltd, but she was returned to her builders as unsatisfactory after one season. After a spell on Belfast Lough on charter, she was purchased in 1885, after the remodelling of part of her hull, by Captain Bob Campbell for the Glasgow to Kilmun route. She is seen here in Campbell colours at Kilcreggan.

In 1888 *Meg Merrilies* was re-boilered and emerged from that with a single funnel. In April of that year Captain Bob Campbell had died and his two sons, Peter and Alex, inherited his steamers but decided that the future for them lay in the Bristol Channel. On 1 January 1889 *Meg* was registered in the name of three nominees of the Caledonian Railway Co., and from 8 May 1889 by the newly formed Caledonian Steam Packet Co. At some stage during the 1890s a fore saloon was added, as seen in this illustration. In 1902, replaced by *Duchess of Montrose*, she was sold to the Leopoldina Railway of Brazil, for whom she ran at Rio de Janeiro as *Maua* until scrapped in 1921.

Madge Wildfire was the second steamer taken over from the Campbell brothers. S. McKnight & Co. of Ayr had built her in 1886. She is seen here off Gourock c.1890.

Madge Wildfire, seen here at the Broomielaw prior to 1902 when her bridge was placed forward of her funnel. She continued to sail on a lunchtime Kilmun to Glasgow cargo service after being purchased by the CSP, although most sailings were from Gourock.

Madge Wildfire in the River Clyde, opposite Dalmuir. By this time she had been fitted with a fore saloon.

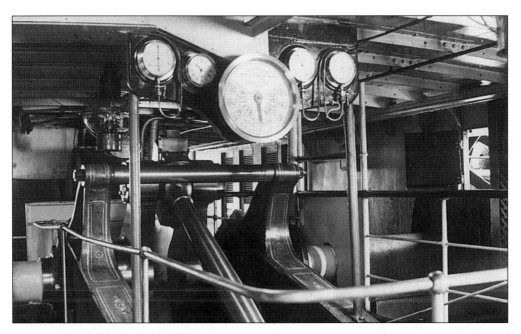

In 1891 *Madge Wildfire* was fitted with a new engine, a tandem compound type similar to that fitted in *Caledonia*.

In 1911 *Madge Wildfire* was sold to Captain A.W. Cameron of Dumbarton for excursion work from Glasgow, and in 1913 to Buchanan Steamers Ltd, for whom she ran as *Isle of Skye*. In 1916 she was taken over by the Admiralty for use as a tender at Invergordon, but returned to the Clyde for what was now Williamson-Buchanan Steamers in 1919. In 1927 she was sold to the Grangemouth & Forth Towing Co. Ltd and ran on the Forth as *Fair Maid*, mainly sailing from Leith to Kirkcaldy and Aberdour and as a tender to liners anchored in the Forth. She also relieved the Queensferry and Granton to Burntisland ferries for overhaul.

During the Second World War *Fair Maid* returned to the Clyde as an Admiralty tender, managed by the Caledonian Steam Packet Co. for the Ministry of War Transport. She was used to tow dumb barges to cargo ships at the Tail of the Bank, and tow them back to Craigendoran. For a week in spring 1944 she relieved *Lucy Ashton* on the Craigendoran to Dunoon run. She is seen here at Craigendoran on VE Day, 8 May 1945. She was scrapped at Troon in December of that year.

Caledonia was the first new steamer to appear for the Caledonian Steam Packet Co. She had been ordered from engine builders Rankin & Blackmore who had sub-contracted the building of the hull to John Reid & Co. of Port Glasgow. She is seen here in original condition prior to 1903.

Caledonia off Gourock after 1903 when her bridge was moved forward of her funnel.

Caledonia was fitted with an unusual type of engine, a two cylinder single crank tandem compound diagonal, as seen here. In 1893 she was experimentally converted to burn oil fuel, but this was not a success and she reverted to coal firing.

Caledonia departing Gourock, again after her bridge had been moved forward of the funnel. From April 1917 to April 1919 she was used as a minesweeper, and for a time reportedly carried troops from Le Havre up the Seine to Paris. She resumed Clyde service in November 1919.

Caledonia spent much of her career on the Holy Loch service and is seen here in the 1923-1924 'Tartan lum' colours approaching Ardnadam Pier in that loch.

Caledonia at the end of her final season, off Kirn on 9 September 1933. She was sold for scrapping at Barrow at the end of that year.

Above: Galatea was a fine two-funnelled steamer similar to *Ivanhoe*, built by Caird & Co. for the CSP's inaugural season in 1889. She is seen here at Gourock Pier in a postcard view.

Page 28 top: Galatea featured on the cover of an undated, (but published prior to 1902) Caledonian Railway booklet, entitled *Caledonian Routes to the Coast*.

THE CALEDONIAN ROUTES TO THE COAST

SPEED AND COMFORT

Galatea at Dunoon Pier in a postcard view.

The same postcard as before, adapted for a moonlit view.

A good promenade. A deck view of a CSP paddle steamer, probably *Galatea*. (*CRSC Archive*)

A stern view of *Galatea*. The captain has his hand on the engine room telegraph, ready to reduce speed to avoid the encroaching yacht. *(A. Ernest Glen Collection)*

Galatea at Craigmore Pier.

Above: The machinery of *Galatea*. (*A. Ernest Glen Collection*)

Right: By 1903 *Galatea* needed a new boiler, but this work was not done and she was laid up at Gourock and never sailed again.

In summer 1906 *Galatea* was sold to Italian owners Soc. Anon di Navigazione Tirrenia (no connection with the present day ferry operator Tirrenia) and sailed for them from Genoa to Monte Carlo, in grey hull as seen here, until sold for scrapping at Palermo in 1912. She seems little altered apart from the erection of sun canopies over the upper deck and bridge. (*G.E. Langmuir Collection, Mitchell Library*)

On 30 April 1890, the CSP took over services from Wemyss Bay from Gillies & Campbell, and to serve this pier another three steamers entered the fleet. *Marchioness of Breadalbane* was the first to be launched, on 15 April, again from the yard of John Reid. Like *Caledonia*, she had been ordered from Rankin & Blackmore, who had sub-contracted the hull. She was ahead of her time, in that her bridge was placed forward of the funnel. She, with her sister *Marchioness of Bute*, was a copy of *Caledonia* with the same tandem compound machinery, but with the bridge forward of the funnel from building. *Marchioness of Breadalbane* is seen here at Gourock.

Marchioness of Breadalbane leaving Rothesay. In the early 1890s she was in service year-round on the Gourock to Rothesay service.

A stern view of *Marchioness of Breadalbane*. From the mid-1890s she was also on the Wemyss Bay to Millport service. In May 1917 she was requisitioned for use as a minesweeper, and did not return to Gourock until 2 May 1919.

Marchioness of Breadalbane in the colours carried from 1925 onwards, with buff funnel with black top. She continued in the Wemyss Bay to Millport service. She is seen here arriving at Dunoon.

Marchioness of Breadalbane in LMS colours with her fore-saloon boarded up for winter service.

Marchioness of Breadalbane departing Rothesay. From November 1933 she replaced the now withdrawn *Caledonia* on the Kilmun service. She remained in service until 18 April 1935. In June 1935 she was sold to the Redcliffe Shipping Company of Hull, who had also operated the former MacBrayne *Fusilier*. In summer 1935 she operated out of East Anglian ports, and in the first part of summer 1936 out of Newcastle, and later that summer out of Lowestoft. In 1937 she was sold to Germany for breaking up.

Marchioness of Bute was an almost identical sister to *Marchioness of Breadalbane* and was launched from Reid's yard on 6 May 1891. She served the Gourock to Rothesay route and from 1895 was on a Wemyss Bay-Rothesay-Tighnabruiach service, including in her roster an afternoon round Bute cruise.

Marchioness of Bute (left) and *Marchioness of Lorne* (right) at Wemyss Bay. *Marchioness of Bute* also served on occasion on the Wemyss Bay to Millport route, and is here at the Millport berth. In June 1908 she was sold to David Nicol of Dundee for service on the Tay. (*CRSC Archive*)

Marchioness of Bute at Newburgh on the Tay. She commenced operating from Dundee to Perth, calling at Newburgh, on 10 July 1908. She also sailed to Leith, Montrose and Lunan Bay, and to the Bell Rock. In 1909 she paid a visit to London for a Naval Review on the Thames and in 1915 she was requisitioned for use as a minesweeper and was sold to the Admiralty in October 1917. In 1919 she was used as a hospital ship as part of the fleet of paddle steamers which sailed for the White Sea in support of the White Russians. When she returned from there she was laid up at Inverkeithing and was sold for scrapping in January 1923.

Duchess of Hamilton was the third steamer of 1890. She was a larger and more luxurious steamer than the two Marchionesses, and was designed for the Ardrossan to Arran service, the Caledonian Railway having reached Ardrossan Montgomerie Pier in May of that year. *Duchess of Hamilton* was built by Denny of Dumbarton and had reportedly originally been ordered for an Australian company as the new *Ozone* (*Ozone* had been a steamer built by Denny for Huddart Parker of Melbourne in 1886), designed by Morton & Williamson, the Williamson of that company being Captain James Williamson, marine Superintendent of the Caledonian Railway, although that was a subterfuge to prevent word of her building leaking out to the rival GSWR. She was the first Clyde steamer to have the promenade deck extended to the bow. She had two-crank compound machinery similar to that installed in *Galatea*. She is seen here in an official Caledonian Railway postcard.

Another official CR postcard, posted at Largs in 1906, this time of *Duchess of Hamilton* on a stormy day off Ardrossan. The message on the reverse of the card reads 'Mary, Papa and I are sailing round Arran and Ailsa (Craig). Rough and Wet….'. An enlarged copy of this card was on display in the dining saloon of the turbine *Duchess of Hamilton* in the 1960s.

W.R.&S. 30948. DUCHESS OF HAMILTON AT KEPPEL PIER, MILLPORT.

1908.
EXCURSIONS
From ROTHESAY

By the CALEDONIAN STEAMERS.

THE SEASON'S PROGRAMME IN A NUTSHELL.

Steamer Leaves at	EXCURSIONS.	Return about	Cabin.	F.Sal.
P.M. 9.40	**LOCH LOMOND TOUR (Daily)** - -	P.M. 5.50	6/-	4/10
A.M. 10.0	**ROUND THE LOCHS** - - - - MONDAYS, WEDNESDAYS, and FRIDAYS (20th and 22nd July excepted)	P.M. 6.0	3/6	2/6
A.M. 10.0	**Round ARRAN and AILSA CRAIG** - TUESDAYS and THURSDAYS (21st July excepted)	P.M. 6.0	2/6	2/-
A.M. 10.45	**Largs, Millport, and Kilchattan Bay** - Via WEMYSS BAY DAILY	P.M. 3.50	1/-	—
A.M. 10.45	**WEMYSS BAY and GOUROCK Circular Tour** (Steamer and Coach) DAILY	P.M. 3.0	2/-	—
A.M. 10.45	**KILCHATTAN CIRCULAR TOUR** - - (Steamer and Coach) DAILY	P.M. 2.0	2/-	—
A.M. 11.10	**ARRAN, via the Kyles of Bute** - - DAILY EXCEPT SATURDAYS	P.M. 4.30	2/6	2/-
A.M. 11.10	**ARRAN and *ARDROSSAN** (via Carroch Head) - SATURDAYS ONLY * Arran only, Saturday, 18th July	P.M. 5.30	2/6	2/-
12.15p (Ex. Sats.) 12.0 n (Sats.only)	**GOUROCK and WEMYSS BAY Circular Tour** (Steamer and Coach) DAILY	P.M. 4.0	2/-	—
P.M. 2.50	**To LARGS and MILLPORT** - - Via WEMYSS BAY DAILY	P.M. 6.0	1/-	—

For full particulars see Excursion Programmes, to be had free on application at the Caledonian Office on the Pier or on board the Steamers.

CALEDONIAN STEAM PACKET COMPANY, LIMITED,
302 BUCHANAN STREET, GLASGOW, July, 1908.

M'Corquodale & Co. Ltd., Glasgow, London, &c.

Above: After *Duchess of Argyll* appeared in 1906, *Duchess of Hamilton* was reboiled and then used on excursion services and rail-connection services from Gourock, until requisitioned in February 1915. She is seen here at Keppel Pier.

Left: A 1908 CSP excursion programme from Rothesay.

Right: Details of Arrochar sailings by *Duchess of Hamilton* in the summer 1911 Programme of Excursions.

Below: Duchess of Hamilton as a minesweeper at Southampton in 1915. On 29 November 1915 she sank after hitting a mine off Harwich. (*Robin Boyd Collection*)

Excursion to ARROCHAR (Loch-Long)

FOR

LOCH-LOMOND

BY THE

"DUCHESS OF HAMILTON"

(DAILY)

GOING.		a.m.	Sats. only. a.m.	RETURNING.		Sats. only. p.m.	Ex. Sats p m	Sats only. p m
Kilchattan Bay ...lve.		a7 10	11 15	Tarbet—				
Millport (Old Pier) ,,		a7 38	10 55	(Coach) ...lve.		...	2 15	5 10
Largs ... ... ,,		8 7	10 50	Arrochar—				
Wemyss Bay ... ,,		9 0	...	(Coach) ...arr.		...	2 35	5 30
Rothesay ... ... ,,		9 45	12 15	(Steamer) ...lve.		12 40	2 45	5 35
Craigmore ... ,,		9 50	12 20	Lochgoilhead ... ,,		...	...	6 30
Innellan ... ... ,,		10 10	12 40	Gourock ... ...arr.		1 55	4 20	7 55
Dunoon ... ... ,,		10 25	12 55	Greenock (Prin. P.) ,,		2 10	4 35	8 10
Kirn ... ... ,,		10 30	1 0	Kirn ... ... ,,		2 15	5 8	8 40
Hunter's Quay ... ,,		...	1 5	Dunoon ... ... ,,		2 20	5 8	8 45
Gourock ... ... ,,		10 47	2 0	Innellan ... ... ,,		2 35	5 25	9 0
Greenock (Prin. P.) ,,		11 0	2 45	Craigmore ... ,,		2 55	5 50	9 20
Lochgoilhead ... ,,		...	4 20	Rothesay ... ... ,,		3 0	5 55	9 25
Arrochar—				Wemyss Bay ... ,,		5 10	7 0	...
(Steamer) arr.		12 30	5 15	Largs ... ... ,,		4 37	7 40	10b10
(Coach) ...lve.		1 15	...	Millport (Old Pier) ,,		4 0	8 2	10b45
Tarbet ,, ...arr.		1 35	...	Kilchattan Bay ... ,,		4 30	8 25	11b10

a 5 minutes earlier on Mondays.   *b* Passengers change at Craigmore.

FARES (excluding Pier Dues at Arrochar, and Coach Fare between Arrochar and Tarbet.)

FROM		Cabin	St'ge	FROM		Cabin	St'ge
Kilchattan Bay ...							
Millport	}	2/6	2/-	Innellan	}	2/6	2/-
Wemyss Bay ...				Dunoon			
Rothesay & Craigmore				Kirn			

Tickets available during the Season, with liberty to break the journey at any Station or place on the Route.

For full particulars of Loch-Lomond Tour see the Companies' Excursion Programme, which may be had at the Companies' Offices or on board the Steamers.

Marchioness of Lorne followed in 1891 from Russell & Co. of Port Glasgow. She was of similar dimensions to the two preceding Marchionesses and was designed for winter service on the Arran run, and is seen here as such, with winter boarding on her saloon windows. She again had engines by Rankin & Blackmore of an unusual type; triple expansion with two cranks, i.e. a twin tandem type, with a high pressure cylinder and a medium pressure cylinder on one crank, and a high pressure cylinder and a low pressure on the other.

Marchioness of Lorne across the end of the pier in Rothesay, with *Columba* and *Lord of the Isles* (*II*) on the outer berths and *Marchioness of Bute* in the inner harbour.

Marchioness of Lorne (left) and *Caledonia* (right) at Wemyss Bay. She served out of Wemyss Bay in the summer months, offering excursions and serving Millport.

Marchioness of Lorne departing from Rothesay.

Marchioness of Lorne in Lamlash Bay with the Channel Fleet anchored in the background. Like the remainder of the CSP fleet, she was requisitioned for use as a minesweeper in the 1914-1918 conflict. She was used in the eastern Mediterranean, based at Malta, and, for a time, Port Said. On return from war service she lay in Bowling Harbour for a considerable time and was broken up at Dumbarton in December 1923.

In 1895, *Duchess of Rothesay* joined the fleet, the first CSP steamer to be built at the yard of J&G Thomson at Clydebank. Her hull was based on that of *Slieve Bearnagh*, which had been built by them the previous year for the Belfast & County Down Railway for Belfast Lough services. She had conventional two-cylinder compound machinery with two cranks. She served initially for a short period in the 1895 season from Ardrossan to Arran, and then on rail connected services from Gourock and Wemyss Bay, and in alternate weeks, to Rothesay. When *Ivanhoe* had become a full member of the CSP fleet in 1897, she took her place on the Arran via the Kyles run. In 1909 she was replaced by *Duchess of Hamilton* on the Arran via Kyles run and resumed serving Rothesay. In the peak seasons of 1911 and 1914 she was on the Ardrossan to Arran run as second ship to *Duchess of Argyll*.

Duchess of Rothesay racing *Waverley* for Rothesay, seen off Toward. She was known in pre-1914 days as 'The Cock of the Walk' and carried a small weathercock at the top of her mast for a time. On 10 September 1897, she was used as a royal yacht by the Duke and Duchess of York at the opening of Cessnock Dock at Govan, in 1907 similarly by the Prince and Princess of Wales at the opening of Rothesay Dock at Clydebank, and again in 1914 by them, now as King George V and Queen Mary, to sail from the Fairfield yard at Govan to see the battleship *Ramillies* under construction at Beardmores at Dalmuir.

Duchess of Rothesay in a photograph from the CP booklet *Caledonian Routes to the Coast*. (*CRSC Archive*)

The first class saloon, on the main deck aft, of *Duchess of Rothesay* from the above booklet. (*CRSC Archive*)

The dining saloon, on the lower deck aft, of *Duchess of Rothesay*, from the same booklet. (*CRSC Archive*)

Looking aft, a deck view from the same booklet. (*CRSC Archive*)

In late 1915 *Duchess of Rothesay* was, like her fleetmates, requisitioned for war service as a minesweeper, and renamed *Duke of Rothesay*. In that capacity she towed a downed Zeppelin, *L15*, into Margate, and assisted in the saving of fourteen ships.

After her return from war, on 1 June 1919, prior to going for refit, she sank at her moorings at Merklands Wharf because mooring ropes had not been slackened to allow for the falling tide, and consequently she canted over and filled with water. The ropes eventually broke and she settled on the river bed. She was raised on 27 July and refitted, re-entering service on 29 March 1920.

Duchess of Rothesay in 1923 with the so-called Tartan funnel colours (yellow, red and black). These were unpopular with the travelling public and only lasted for two years.

From 1926, *Duchess of Rothesay* was on the 10.25 a.m. all-piers service from Greenock to Auchenlochan in the Kyles of Bute, with a morning up run from Rothesay, a couple of tea-time returns to Dunoon and an evening single trip back to Rothesay where she spent the night. She is seen here with a full load of passengers. She is seen here arriving at Dunoon.

Duchess of Rothesay at Keppel Pier on 20 August 1936.

By the late thirties, *Duchess of Rothesay* was being surpassed by the new steamers but still had a loyal following. She is seen here at Greenock Princes Pier with the 1935 *Marchioness of Lorne*.

On certain days during the summer of 1939, *Duchess of Rothesay* returned to her pre-1914 route to Arran via the Kyles. She again saw war service as a minesweeper in the Second World War, and, from April 1942 as an accommodation ship at Brightlingsea. Worn out, at the age of fifty-one, she did not return to the Clyde after the war and was scrapped in Holland in 1946. This was the end for one of the CSP's fastest steamers.

The Royal Route
TO THE
ISLAND OF ARRAN,
BY THE
"IVANHOE,"

Above: Ivanhoe was purchased by the CSP from the Frith (sic) of Clyde Steam Packet Co. in May 1897. She had been built by D. & W. Henderson & Co. as a revolutionary 'teetotal steamer' for that company, part owned by Captain James Williamson, in 1880, and had served on the Arran via the Kyles run, starting her sailings at Helensburgh each day. Her machinery was of the two-cylinder single crank simple oscillating type. She is seen here at Lamlash with *Guinevere*, probably prior to 1885 when the latter was transferred to a Broomielaw to Rothesay run.

Right: An 1888 advertisement for *Ivanhoe* from *Pollok's Dictionary of the Clyde*.

Is universally conceded to be the Finest Excursion on the Clyde, connecting with NORTH BRITISH, GLASGOW AND SOUTH WESTERN, and CALEDONIAN RAILWAYS, *via* Helensburgh, Princes Pier, and Wemyss Bay.

RETURN FARES.

From Helensburgh or Greenock, Saloon, 3s. 6d. ; Fore Saloon, 2s. 6d.
From Dunoon, etc., - - - ,, 3s. od. ; ,, 2s. od.
From Rothesay, - - - ,, 2s. 6d. ; ,, 1s. 6d.
RETURN TICKETS to Arran, per Rail and Steamer, may be had at the Railway Stations in Edinburgh and Glasgow.

FRITH OF CLYDE STEAM PACKET CO. LTD.,
75 BUCHANAN STREET, GLASGOW.

49

Ivanhoe made a ferry call at Corrie, seen here, on her regular Arran via the Kyles run.

Broomielaw, Glasgow (off down the Water)

In 1911 *Ivanhoe* was sold to a new company, the Firth of Clyde Steam Packet Ltd, and commenced operating from the Broomielaw to Rothesay. Her funnels were painted white and, from 1912, her funnels received a narrow black top.

Above: Ivanhoe's paddle boxes were painted black by her new owners.

Opposite: Ivanhoe in 1894. From 1888 she had been calling at Gourock, in the year prior to the completion of the railway. From 23 March (Good Friday) 1894 until 22 May she operated the Liverpool to Manchester sailings on the Manchester Ship Canal, and took part in the official opening on 21 May. In 1897, with her Arran sailings affected by competition from the GSWR's *Neptune*, the Frith of Clyde Co. closed down and she was sold to the CSP, in fact from Captain James Williamson's left hand to his right. In 1897 she operated rail-connected services from Gourock. From 1898 to 1905 she was again on excursion services, sailing on Mondays to Arrochar, on Tuesdays and Thursdays to Millport, continuing on Tuesdays round Arran and on Thursdays round Ailsa Craig, on Wednesdays and Fridays Round the Lochs, and sailing on Saturdays as a general relief steamer.

51

Ivanhoe at Rothesay, with *Iona* arriving, *Eagle III* behind her, and *Duchess of Rothesay* at the far end of a pier jam-packed with humanity.

Above: In 1914 *Ivanhoe* was sold to Turbine Steamers Ltd, but continued to sail from Broomielaw, initially to Rothesay, and in July and August to Lochgoilhead with a non-landing cruise to Arrochar. She is seen here in June of that year. On the outbreak of war she was laid up, but in 1916, with eight of their steamers away at war, she was chartered by the CSP, serving until September 1919. She was then laid up in the West Harbour at Greenock until sold for scrapping at Dumbarton a year later. (*A. Ernest Glen*)

Left: Duchess of Montrose came in 1902 from John Brown, who by then had taken over J. & G. Thomson. She was similar to *Duchess of Rothesay*, although smaller, and had four-cylinder two-crank triple expansion engines, like those fitted in *Marchioness of Lorne*. She was initially on an Ayr excursion roster, but later moved to rail-connected services on the upper firth and is see here arriving at Gourock.

Duchess of Montrose at Wemyss Bay, showing the pier buildings.

Passengers boarding *Duchess of Montrose* in a postcard view at an unusually quiet Rothesay Pier.

Above: Duchess of Montrose was called up for trooping and minesweeping. On 18 March 1917 she was lost while minesweeping off the Belgian coast in preparation for a British raid. (*CRSC Collection*)

Duchess of Fife was built in 1903 by Fairfield of Govan, the first Clyde steamer they had ever built, and was – except for minor differences – similar to *Duchess of Montrose*, e.g. she had a raked funnel and larger paddle boxes. She was destined to have a long career of some fifty years on the Firth of Clyde and serve in, and survive, both World Wars. She had two-crank triple expansion machinery like *Duchess of Montrose*. She took less than six months to build.

Duchess of Fife in a pre-1913 postcard view at Wemyss Bay, with a large crowd on board and many more passengers waiting to embark. With the new post-*Titanic* regulations in 1913, she was fitted with an additional lifeboat aft on the promenade deck. In spring 1916 she was requisitioned by the Admiralty and became the minesweeper HMS *Duchess*. She returned to peacetime duty in 1919.

Duchess of Fife in the tartan funnel condition, in 1923-1924. (*A. Ernest Glen Collection*)

Duchess of Fife in LMS colours with a black top to her funnel. The additional lifeboat fitted in 1913 can be seen in this shot.

In summer 1936, *Duchess of Fife* ran aground off Kirn. Behind her to the left is the LNER steamer *Marmion*. (*From a postcard published by the* Dunoon Observer)

From 1937 *Duchess of Fife* was transferred to the Wemyss Bay to Millport and Kilchattan Bay service. She is seen here leaving Millport.

Duchess of Fife on Lamont's slipway undergoing refit.

Duchess of Fife was again requisitioned in 1939 for use as a minesweeper, and made three trips to Dunkirk to assist in the evacuation in 1940. From 1941 she was based at Port Edgar on the Forth as a minesweeper training ship and tender, returning to the Clyde in 1946. She is seen here waiting to go into Lamont's yard for reconditioning.

In 1947 *Duchess of Fife* was fitted with a wheelhouse, prior to the remainder of the CSP fleet, and she is seen here in 1952 in Rothesay Bay.

Duchess of Fife arriving at Gourock in winter-boarded condition post-1948, with the stern of *Marchioness of Lorne* to the left.

Opposite below: Duchess of Fife lying in Greenock's Albert Harbour after her withdrawal. In BR days her hull had two gold lines round it. (*A. Ernest Glen, courtesy of Bruce Peter*)

Duchess of Fife arriving at Rothesay. With the advent of the Maids and the ABC car ferries in 1953, there was no place for her in a modernized CSP fleet, and she was withdrawn in June 1953 and sold for scrapping.

Denny of Dumbarton had built the pioneer turbine steamers *King Edward* and *Queen Alexandra* for James Williamson's brother John and his company Turbine Steamers in 1901 and 1902. In 1906 the CSP took delivery of its first turbine, *Duchess of Argyll*, from Denny. She initially operated the Ardrossan Montgomerie Pier to Arran service, in fierce competition with the GSWR turbine of the same year, *Atalanta*. She is seen here off Kings Cross, which was a ferry call north of Whiting Bay. Her main deck was originally open forward like those of the paddle steamers.

Duchess of Argyll in 1907 with the main deck open at the bow. This area was normally used by the crew for rope-handling. (*A. Ernest Glen Collection*)

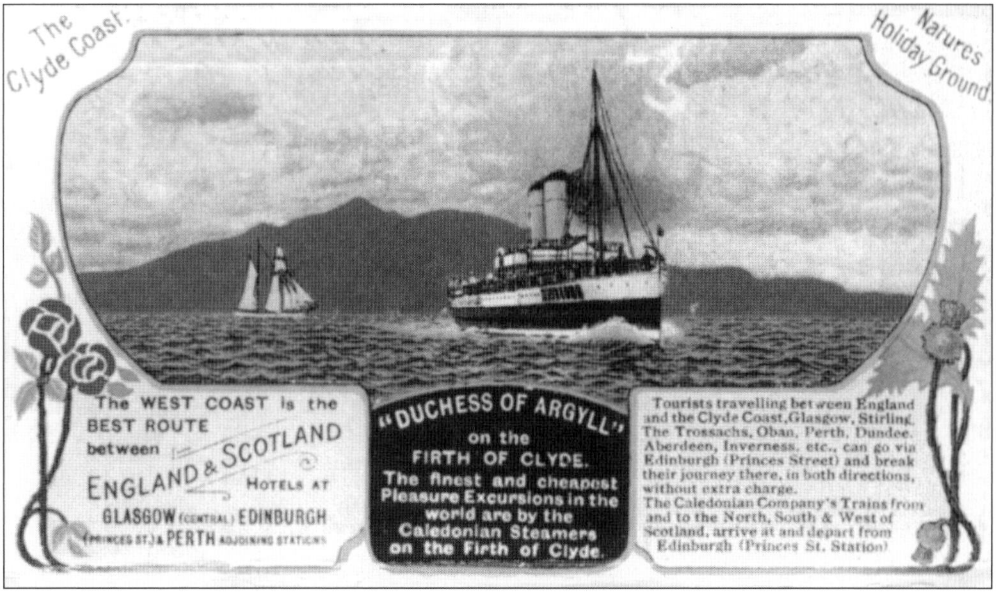

A Caledonian Railway publicity view of *Duchess of Argyll*, taken from a CR folding map. She never actually operated in this condition with large windows in the fore saloon and plated up at the bow.

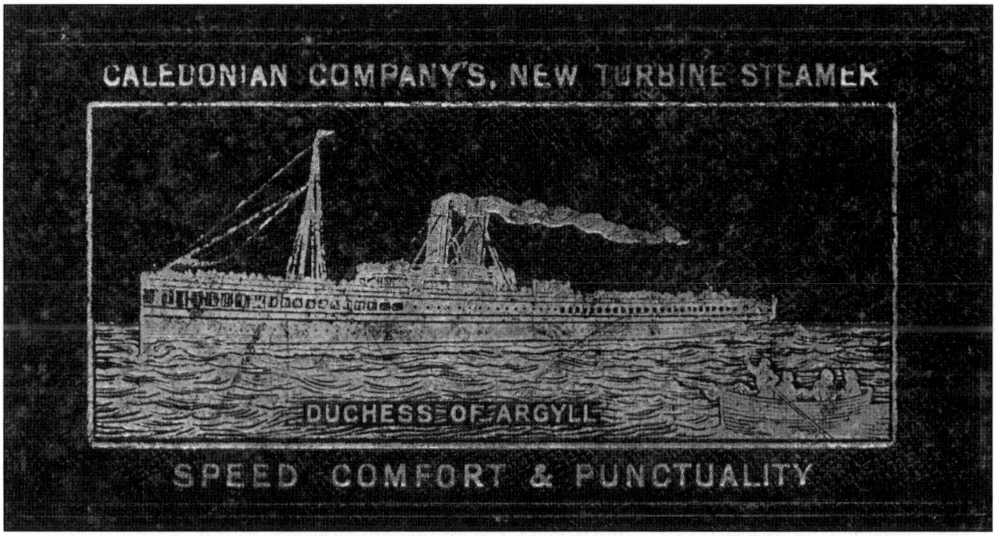

A gold-blocked engraving of *Duchess of Argyll* from the cover of the same map, showing her with the main deck open forward and the slogan 'speed, comfort, & punctuality'. The caption on the map itself states 'Pleasure sailing on the Clyde is the finest and cheapest in the world. The Caledonian Routes are the shortest, quickest, and best'.

A stern view of *Duchess of Argyll* departing Ardrossan in her original condition. In 1908 the CSP and GSWR came to a pooling agreement for the Arran route, and in that year *Duchess of Argyll* was laid up. Each company henceforth operated the route in alternate years until 1914.

Duchess of Argyll off Lamlash in her original condition, but with her fore saloon windows boarded up to counter winter storms.

In 1910 and 1911 *Duchess of Argyll* was earmarked for use as a relief steamer on the Stranraer to Larne service and her bow was plated in and her fore saloon windows replaced by portholes. In 1910 she did not sail on the cross-channel route but, in June 1911, she offered a day cruise from Larne and Stranraer round Ailsa Craig, on Saturday 10 June, and relieved *Princess Maud* from 12-17 June. *Princess Maud* was undergoing repairs at that time after an altercation with the quay at Larne.

Duchess of Argyll in 1910-1914 condition at Brodick with a flotilla of torpedo boats in the bay. During the First World War she was used as a transport across the English Channel from February 1915 to April 1919. On one occasion in 1917 she towed the Williamson paddle steamer *Queen Empress* into Boulogne after the latter had been involved in a collision.

An 'On Board' postcard of *Duchess of Argyll* in the 1923-1924 'tartan funnel' colour scheme. From 1919 she had been placed on the Arran via the Kyles run, which she served until 1935.

Above: The Arran via the Kyles run involved a ferry call at Corrie, where *Duchess of Argyll* is seen in this view. *(CRSC Archive)*

Left: A deck view of *Duchess of Argyll* on the cover of the 1925 CSP timetable.

Right: The timetable for the Arran via the Kyles run, from the 1925 CSP summer timetable.

Below: Duchess of Argyll dressed overall. In 1936 she took over the Inveraray service three days a week, with passengers having an option of a bus return to Dunoon, the 'famed Lock Eck tour', and also served Campbeltown three days a week, thus replacing both *King George V* and *Queen Alexandra*.

To ARRAN

Via KYLES OF BUTE, returning via GARROCH HEAD.

By Turbine Steamer "DUCHESS OF ARGYLL"

(OR OTHER STEAMER).

DAILY (Ceases after 12th September).

	a.m.	a.m.			p.m.	
Edinburgh (Princes St.) ....dep.	..	6 55		Whiting Bay ....dep.	2 30	
				Lamlash .... "	2 50	
Glasgow (St Enoch) via Prin. Pr.	8 5	..	Arran	Brodick .... "	3 10	
Glasgow (Cent.) { via Gourock	8 0	..		Corrie .... "	3 30	
{ via Wem. Bay	..	9 30		Tighnabruaich ....arr.	6*45	
				Rothesay .... "	4 25	
Greenock (Princes Pier) ..dep.	8 50	..		Craigmore .... "	4 20	
Gourock .... "	9 8	..		Wemyss Bay .... "	5 0	
Kirn .... "	9 22	..				
Dunoon .... "	9 30	..		Largs .... "	..	5*55
Innellan .... "	9*37	..		Millport (Keppel) .... "	..	6*13
Millport (Old Pier)....... "	8*30	..		Do. (Old Pier) .... "	..	6*20
Do. (Keppel) .... "	8*37	..		Innellan .... "	..	4*55
Largs .... "	10/0	..		Dunoon .... "	..	5 30
				Kirn .... "	..	5 35
Wemyss Bay .... "	10 38			Gourock .... "	..	5 50
Craigmore .... "	11 0			Greenock (Princes Pier) .. "	..	6 5
Rothesay .... "	11 5					
Tighnabruaich ....arr.	11 45			Glasgow (Central)		
Arran { Corrie .... "	12 50			via Wemyss Bay ....arr.	6*14	..
{ Brodick .... "	1 10			" Gourock .... "	..	6 56
{ Lamlash .... "	1 30			Glasgow (St.En.) via Prin.Pr.	..	7 2
{ Whiting Bay .... "	1 55					
				Edinburgh (Princes St.) ..arr.	8 12	..

b Passengers change at Wemyss Bay. On 23rd and 30th July, 3rd August, and daily from 1st September, Passengers leave at 9-25 a.m. and change at Rothesay.
c Passengers change at Wemyss Bay. Commencing 2nd September, Passengers leave Millport (Old Pier) at 7-5 a.m. and Keppel at 7-12 a.m., Mondays excepted, and Millport (Old Pier) at 7 2 a.m. and Keppel at 7-27 a.m. on Mondays.
d Arrives at 6-29 p.m. on Saturdays.
e Passengers change at Rothesay. On Saturdays arrives Tighnabruaich 7-30 p.m.
f On 1st August, Passengers leave Largs at 8-55 a.m. and join Arran Steamer at Wemyss Bay.
h Passengers change at Craigmore.
k Passengers change at Wemyss Bay. On Saturdays arrive Largs 6-10, Keppel 6-28 and Millport (Old Pier) 6-35 p.m. Saturdays excepted, commencing 1st September, arrives Largs at 6-40 p.m., Keppel at 7-3 p.m. and Millport at 7-10 p.m.

RETURN FARES.

From						1st Class and Cabin	3rd Class and Cabin	3rd Class Steerage
Edinburgh				..	..	22/4	14/-	12/8½
Glasgow (Central and St. Enoch)			..	..	..	9/2½	7/-	5/8½
							Cabin	Steerage
Greenock }	..	..	..	..	..	..	5/3	3/9
Gourock }								
Kirn }								
Dunoon }								
Innellan }	..	..	..	..	..	..	4/6	3/-
Largs }								
Millport }								
Wemyss Bay }								
Craigmore }								
Rothesay }	..	..	..	..	..	..	3/9	3/-
Tighnabruaich }								

Printed in Scotland by JOHN HORN, LTD.

HEALTH AND PLEASURE
CRUISES

While Spending Your Leisure — Enjoy Health and Pleasure

The "Reel" Mackay   A Grand

Scotch Cruise

'Mid Scotland's Rugged Grandeur, to

LOCH FYNE

(via the Kyles of Bute).   Passengers have option of Time
Ashore at

TIGHNABRUAICH

(rejoining Steamer on return) on

Saturday, 23rd July

By the "Reel" Scotch Cruiser
" DUCHESS OF ARGYLL "

Leaving

Dunoon	6-10 p.m.	Largs	7-15 p.m.
Gourock	6-30 p.m.	Rothesay	7-45 p.m.

Novelty Competition

(a) Ladies to find Mr. McHaggis. (b) Gents. to find Miss McPurritch
Special Prizes for the best Scotch Turns
Special Engagement—'THE ORLO TRIO'—*Special Engagement*
Highland Dancing Display by Crack Troup of Speciality Dancers

Dancing   —   Community Singing

Led by "THE CLANSMEN." Directed by T. Wilson
A Non-Stop Feast of Scotch Fare

2/2   CRUISE FARE   2/2
JUVENILES HALF-PRICE

Tickets on Sale at Piers on Day of Cruise.   Book Early
Buses in connection for Saltcoats, Kilbirnie, Glasgow, etc.

It's an H.P. Cruise

R.L., 5000/7/38

'Health and Pleasure Cruises' Leaflet, July 1938

2

PLEASE RETAIN THIS BILL FOR REFERENCE

LONDON MIDLAND AND SCOTTISH RAILWAY AND   B 9422 R
THE CALEDONIAN STEAM PACKET COMPANY, LTD

Friday, 17th August

Special
Up-River Cruise

To View

No. 534.

(THE NEW CUNARDER)

By Turbine Steamer

"DUCHESS OF ARGYLL"

Kilcreggan	- - leave	6.15
Blairmore	- - „	6.30
Dunoon	- - - „	6.45
Gourock	- - - „	7.5
Greenock (Princes Pier)	- „	7.15

Arriving back at Greenock (Princes Pier) about 10.0, Kilcreggan 10.15,
Blairmore 10.30, Dunoon 10.45, Gourock 11.0 p.m.

FARE	- - - -	1/9

CONDITIONS OF ISSUE OF EXCURSION TICKETS AND OTHER TICKETS AT LESS
THAN ORDINARY FARE —These Tickets are issued subject to the Notices and Conditions
shown in the Company's Current Time Tables

August, 1934.   J. BALLANTYNE, Chief Officer for Scotland.
E.R.O. 53302.

ZD—14 8 34—No. 1—2 SPN   JOHN HORN

Above left: A handbill for an evening cruise to Loch Fyne in 1938 by *Duchess of Argyll*.

Above right: A handbill for an up-river evening cruise by *Duchess of Argyll* in 1934 to see the new Cunarder No.534 (which was to become RMS *Queen Mary*) being built at John Brown at Clydebank.

Duchess of Argyll, as seen here, had her upper deck opened up to passengers in her later years.

Opposite below: Duchess of Argyll leaving Kirn Pier. After 1945 she was on the Greenock Princes Pier to Rothesay service, which would have involved calls at Kirn.

Duchess of Argyll remained on the Clyde during the Second World War, initially operating the Gourock to Dunoon service and later acting as a tender to troopships lying at the Tail of the Bank. In 1938 she had been fitted with a crosstrees and is seen here in Rothesay Bay.

Duchess of Argyll at Kilmun in wartime condition. (*A. Ernest Glen Collection*)

A stern view of *Duchess of Argyll* arriving at Gourock.

Duchess of Argyll at Rothesay after 1948, when a wheelhouse was fitted, but still with canvas dodgers on the bridge. She was sold to the Admiralty in February 1952 and the hull used for experimental purposes in Portland Harbour until 1969. In 1970 she was scrapped at Newhaven. (*J.T.A. Brown*)

During the First World War and until 1920, with all of the CSP steamers away at war, services were maintained by a variety of chartered vessels. These included Williamson's *Benmore*, seen here on Glasgow Autumn Holiday, Monday 27 September 1919, her last day in CSP service. At this time she was on the Millport service but had previously been on the Kilmun route. (*CRSC Archive*)

MacBrayne's *Chevalier* was also chartered during the war and again in 1920. She is seen here at Kilchattan Bay on 17 July 1920. Other chartered vessels in this period included *Fusilier, Ivanhoe, Glencoe, Lochinvar, Mountaineer* and *Lord of the Isles*. *Chevalier* finished her charter in early August 1920. (*Courtesy Wm Lind*)

Three
LMS-Owned
1923-1947

In 1924, the former GSWR paddler *Glen Sannox* was worn out and in need of reboilering. It was decided to scrap her and to build a turbine steamer to replace her. The new *Glen Sannox* came from Denny's yard at Dumbarton in 1925, and was almost an identical copy of *Duchess of Argyll* completed twenty years earlier. She was owned by the LMSR, like her predecessor, and as such, was legally unable to sail to Campbeltown or Loch Fyne ports. She could be told from *Duchess of Argyll* by her narrower funnel tops.

Top: Glen Sannox performed the service from Ardrossan to the three Arran piers of Brodick, Lamlash, and Whiting Bay until early 1936.

Middle: Glen Sannox at Brodick in a postcard view.

Right: From her initial season, *Glen Sannox* offered cruises during her midday lay-over at Whiting Bay, as seen in this page from the 1925 CSP timetable.

MID-DAY SAILINGS
(WEATHER FAVOURABLE)

BY NEW TURBINE STEAMER

"GLEN SANNOX"
FROM

ARDROSSAN AND ARRAN.

				DEPSET. a.m.	ARRIVE. p.m.
ARDROSSAN (Winton Pier)	..	..	..	10 10	4 40
BRODICK	..	..	..	11 5	3 40
LAMLASH	..	..	..	11 35	3 15
WHITING BAY	..	..	..	12 0n	2 45

JUNE.

Thursday,	11th	..	AYR (allowing about 50 minutes ashore).
Monday,	15th	..	ROUND ARRAN.
Friday,	28th	..	ROUND AILSA CRAIG.

JULY.

Tuesday,	7th	..	CAMPBELTOWN LOCH.
Friday,	10th	..	AYR (allowing about 50 minutes ashore).
Monday,	13th	..	ROUND ARRAN.
Friday,	17th	..	CAMPBELTOWN LOCH.
Tuesday,	21st	..	ROUND ARRAN.
Wednesday,	22nd	..	AYR (allowing about 50 minutes ashore).
Friday,	24th	..	ROUND AILSA CRAIG.

AUGUST.

Friday,	7th	..	AYR (allowing about 50 minutes ashore).
Wednesday,	12th	..	ROUND ARRAN.
Friday,	14th	..	CAMPBELTOWN LOCH.
Monday,	17th	..	ROUND ARRAN.
Wednesday,	19th	..	AYR (allowing about 50 minutes ashore).
Monday,	24th	..	ROUND AILSA CRAIG.
Friday,	28th	..	ROUND ARRAN.

					Cabin	Steerage
FARES.						
From ARDROSSAN	..	..	..	..	4/6	3/
From ARRAN	..	..	..	..	3/	2 6

SPECIAL EVENING CRUISES FROM ARDROSSAN
DURING JULY AND AUGUST By Turbine Steamer, "Atalanta"

For particulars see Special Posters.

Glen Sannox disembarking passengers at Whiting Bay, with a bus and a line-up of cars and taxis awaiting her arrival.

A three-steamer view of Whiting Bay with *Duchess of Argyll* at the pier, *Glen Sannox* having just left, and *Jeanie Deans* lying off. In 1936, after the introduction of *Marchioness of Graham* on the Ardrossan to Arran service, *Glen Sannox* introduced a new service from Ardrossan to Whiting Bay and Campbeltown. In order to do this her ownership was transferred from the LMSR to the CSP. This helped to replace the sailings of *Queen Alexandra*, which had at the end of the previous year been sold to David MacBrayne Ltd and had become their *Saint Columba*.

Right: A 1937 advertisement for day return fares by these trips to Campbeltown by *Glen Sannox.*

Below: In the early part of September 1939, *Glen Sannox* was on the Stranraer to Larne route for a few days but, apart from that, remained in Clyde service during the war, serving Arran from Fairlie, although she is seen here leaving Gourock.

In 1948, *Glen Sannox* was fitted with a wheelhouse and she remained on the Arran run until the end of the 1953 season. She is seen here laid up in the Albert Harbour, Greenock, in 1952 and she was sold in July 1954 for scrapping at Ghent in Belgium.

1930 saw the arrival of *Duchess of Montrose*, the first of eight new steamers which were to join the fleet in the 1930s. A considerable improvement on *Glen Sannox*, she featured an enclosed promenade deck with an inside observation lounge, and was the first Clyde steamer to be built as a one-class ship. Like the two previous turbine steamers for the company, she was built and engined by William Denny & Bros Ltd of Dumbarton.

Opposite top: A stern three-quarter view of *Duchess of Montrose* leaving Dunoon. She came out in 1930 with a stump mainmast, which was replaced by a full height mainmast in 1934.

Below left: Duchess of Montrose featured on the cover of the CSP summer timetable in the 1930s and late 1950s, in a strangely doctored picture with the sky removed above the rigging lines. This, and the three timetables on the following page, is from the 1932 summer timetable.

Below right: Duchess of Montrose offered evening excursions, such as this one to Largs Illuminations on 19 September 1933.

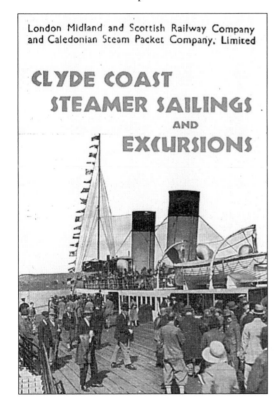

London Midland and Scottish Railway Company and Caledonian Steam Packet Company, Limited

CLYDE COAST
STEAMER SAILINGS
AND
EXCURSIONS

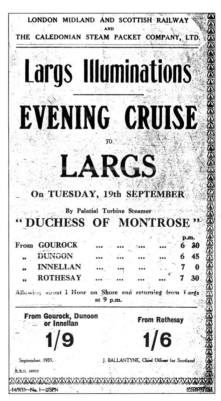

LONDON MIDLAND AND SCOTTISH RAILWAY
AND
THE CALEDONIAN STEAM PACKET COMPANY, LTD.

Largs Illuminations

EVENING CRUISE
TO
LARGS

On TUESDAY, 19th SEPTEMBER

By Palatial Turbine Steamer
"DUCHESS OF MONTROSE"

					p.m.
From GOUROCK	...	...	...	...	6 30
„ DUNOON	...	...	...	...	6 45
„ INNELLAN	...	...	...	...	7 0
„ ROTHESAY	...	...	...	...	7 30

Allowing about 1 Hour on Shore and returning from Largs at 9 p.m.

From Gourock, Dunoon or Innellan	From Rothesay
1/9	**1/6**

September. 1933.   J. BALLANTYNE, Chief Officer for Scotland

R.R.O. 64303

14/9/33—No. 1—2/SPN

75

ROUND THE ISLANDS OF ARRAN and AILSA CRAIG

Going via Kilbrannan Sound and returning via East Side of Arran.
By Palatial Turbine Steamer "DUCHESS OF MONTROSE" (weather favourable)

On TUESDAYS (ceases after 20th September)

STATIONS.	Via Gourock a.m.	Via Wemyss Bay a.m.	STATIONS.	Via Gourock a.m.	Via Wemyss Bay a.m.
Edinburgh (Princes Street) ...Train leaves	...	7 50	Dunoon ....Stnr. leaves	9 20	...
Glasgow (Central) ,,	...	9 30	Innellan ,,	9 25	...
Paisley (Gil. St.) ,,	...	9 42	Rothesay ,,	10 5	...
Port-Glasgow ,,	8 25	10 1	Wemyss Bay ,,	...	10 25
Greenock (Central) ,,	8 33	...			
Do. (West) ,,	8 37	...			
Greenock (P. Pr.) ...Stnr. leaves	8&40	...	Largs ,,	10 55	...
Gourock ,,	9 0	...	Millport (Keppel Pier) ,,	11 10	...

THENCE ROUND THE ISLANDS OF ARRAN and AILSA CRAIG.

	p.m.			p.m.
Millport (Keppel Pier) ...Stnr. arrives	3 55	Gourock ....Stnr. arrives	5 55
Largs ,,	4 10	Greenock (West) ...Train arrives	...
Wemyss Bay ,,	5&10	Do. (Central) ,,	...
Craigmore ,,	4 40	Port-Glasgow ,,	...
Rothesay ,,	5 0	Paisley (Gil. St.) ,,	...
Innellan ,,	5 25	Glasgow (Central) ,,	...
Dunoon ,,	5 40	Edinburgh (Princes Street) ,,	...

b Passengers change at Largs and leave by Steamer at 4.45 p.m. for Wemyss Bay. Exchange Tickets to be had at Ticket Office.
d On return journey Passengers land at Gourock and proceed to destination by connecting train.

RETURN FARES	1st Class & Cabin.	3rd Class & Cabin.	From	1st Class & Cabin.	3rd Class & Cabin.
Edinburgh (Princes Street)	14/9	10/6	Dunoon and Innellan	—	5/-
Glasgow and Paisley	10/-	7/6	Craigmore and Rothesay	—	—
Greenock and Gourock	—	5/6	Wemyss Bay, Largs and Millport	—	4/-

The Tickets are valid on Day of Issue only.

Saturday Afternoon Excursions
ROUND AILSA CRAIG
(Weather permitting)
By Palatial Turbine Steamer "DUCHESS OF MONTROSE" (or other Steamer)
(Ceases after 24th September).

STATIONS.	p.m.	STATIONS.	p.m.
Edinburgh (Prin. St.) ...leave	...	Largs ....arrive	7 45
Glasgow (St. Enoch) ,,	1 43	Wemyss Bay ,,	8&20
Do. (Central) ,,	1 58	Rothesay ,,	8 35
Paisley ,,	...	Craigmore ,,	8 40
Port-Glasgow ,,	...	Gourock ,,	5 20
Greenock (Prin. Pier) ,,	...	Dunoon ,,	9 5
Gourock ,,	...	Paisley ,,	10 49
Dunoon ,,	...	Glasgow (Central) ,,	10 5
Rothesay ,,	...	Do. (St. Enoch) ,,	10&17
Wemyss Bay ,,	3 50	Edinburgh (Prin. St.) ,,	10&48

THENCE ROUND AILSA CRAIG.

b Via Wemyss Bay. e Via Greenock (Princes Pier).
d Passengers join and leave "Duchess of Montrose" at Wemyss Bay.

FARES.		
From	1st Class & Cabin.	3rd Class & Cabin.
Edinburgh	14/9	10/6
Glasgow and Paisley—via Gourock or Greenock	6/9	5/8
via Wemyss Bay	7/9	6/3
Greenock, Gourock, Dunoon, Rothesay and Wemyss Bay	4/-	3/-
Largs	3/-	...

The Tickets are valid on Day of Issue only.

Commences 6th June.
THE ROUND OF THE LOCHS AND THE FIRTH OF CLYDE
By Palatial Turbine Steamer "DUCHESS OF MONTROSE" (or other Steamer)
(Weather favourable)

which includes the Round of the Islands of Bute and Cumbrae, Kyles of Bute, Loch Ridden, Loch Striven, Loch Goil, and Loch Long—is generally conceded to be the most popular excursion on the Clyde. It embraces in one day a wide range and variety of scenery which can only be equalled by spending several days on board the various Excursion Steamers.
Passengers may land at 2.30 p.m. and rejoin Steamer on return from Loch Goil and Loch Lon at 4.45 p.m.

MONDAYS and FRIDAYS only (Friday, 16th September, excepted).
Ceases after 23rd September.

STATIONS.	Via Gourock a.m.	Via Wemyss Bay a.m.	STATIONS.	p.m.
Edinburgh (Princes St.) ...Train leave	...	7 50	*Millport (Old Pier) ...Stnr. arr.	6 15
Glasgow (Central) ,,	...	9 30	† Do. (Keppel Pier) ,,	6 8
Paisley (Gil. St.) ,,	...	9 42	†Largs ,,	5 50
Port-Glasgow ,,	8 25	10 1	Wemyss Bay ,,	5 50
Greenock (West) ,,	8 33	...	Craigmore ,,	5 25
Do. (West) ,,	8 37	...	Rothesay ,,	5 20
Greenock (P. Pr.) ...Stnr. leave	8&40	...	†Innellan ,,	5 5
Gourock ,,	9 0	...	Dunoon ,,	4 45
Dunoon ,,	9 20	...	†Gourock ,,	5 50
Innellan ,,	9 25	...	†Greenock (Prin. Pier) ,,	6 0
Craigmore ,,	9 10	...		
Rothesay ,,	...	9 50	Greenock (West) ...Train arr.	...
Wemyss Bay ,,	...	10 8	Do. (Central) ,,	...
			Port-Glasgow ,,	...
Largs ,,	...	...	Paisley (Gil. St.) ,,	...
Millport ,,	...	10 55	Glasgow (Cent.) ,,	...
(Keppel Pier)	...	11 10	Edinburgh ,,	...
Thence Round the Lochs.				

† Passengers returning to Largs and Millport change at Wemyss Bay.
* Passengers returning to Innellan, Greenock and Gourock change at Dunoon.
a Passengers leave Greenock by Arran Steamer and join "Duchess of Montrose" at Gourock.

RETURN FARES (Valid Day of Issue only).					
From	1st Class & Cabin.	3rd Class & Cabin.	From	1st Class & Cabin.	3rd Class & Cabin.
Edinburgh	14/9	10/6	Dunoon and Innellan	—	5/-
Glasgow and Paisley	10/-	7/6	Craigmore and Rothesay	—	—
Greenock and Gourock	—	5/6	Wemyss Bay, Largs and Millport	—	4/-

Commences 6th June.
Afternoon Excursions
To LOCH GOIL and LOCH LONG (Weather favourable).
By Palatial Turbine Steamer "DUCHESS OF MONTROSE" (or other Steamer).
MONDAYS and FRIDAYS only (Friday, 16th September, excepted).
Ceases after 23rd September.

	noon		Returning	p.m.
aGourock ....Stnr. dep.	12 0	aGourock ,,	4 45
Dunoon ,,	2 0p	Dunoon ,,	5 20
Dunoon ,,	2 30	Dunoon ,,	5 40
Thence to Loch Goil and Loch Long			

a Passengers from and to Gourock change at Dunoon.

RETURN FARES.	
From Gourock	3/-
Rothesay	2/6
Dunoon	2/-

The Tickets are valid on Day of Issue only.

Above right: The sailings of *Duchess of Montrose* in the 1930s were mainly day excursions. On Mondays and Fridays she sailed on 'The round of the Lochs and Firth of Clyde'.

To AYR (commences 15th June)
By Palatial Turbine Steamer "DUCHESS OF MONTROSE"
On WEDNESDAYS (Weather permitting).   Ceases after 21st September.
(Wednesdays, 3rd August and 14th September excepted.)

	a.m.	a.m.		p.m.
Edinburgh (Princes Street)......dep.	...	7 50	Ayr ....dep.	2 45
Glasgow (Central) ,,	...	9 30	Millport (Keppel Pier) ,,	3 55
Paisley (Gilmour Street) ,,	...	9 42	Largs ,,	4 10
Port-Glasgow ,,	8 25	10 1	Wemyss Bay ,,	5&10
Greenock (Central) ,,	8 33	...	Craigmore ,,	4 40
Do. (West) ,,	8 37	...	Rothesay ,,	5 0
Greenock (Princes Pier) ,,	8&40	...	Innellan ,,	5 25
Gourock ,,	9 0	...	Dunoon ,,	5 40
Dunoon ,,	9 20	...	Gourock ,,	5 55
Innellan ,,	9 35	...		
Craigmore ,,	10 10	...	Greenock (West) ,,	...
Rothesay ,,	10 5	...	Do. (Central) ,,	...
Wemyss Bay ,,	...	10 35	Port Glasgow ,,	...
			Paisley (Gilmour Street) ,,	...
Largs ,,	...	10 55	Glasgow (Central) ,,	...
Millport (Keppel Pier) ,,	...	11 10	Edinburgh (Princes Street)... arr.	...
Ayr ,,	...	12 30p		

b Passengers change at Largs and leave by Steamer at 4.45 p.m. for Wemyss Bay. Exchange Tickets to be had at Ticket Office.
d Passengers leave Greenock (Princes Pier) by Arran Steamer and join "Duchess of Montrose" at Gourock.
On return journey Passengers land at Gourock and proceed to destination by connecting train.

RETURN FARES			
From	1st Class & Cabin.	3rd Class & Cabin.	Day Excursion.
Edinburgh (Princes Street)	14/6	10/3	—
Glasgow and Paisley	9/6	7/-	—
Greenock and Gourock	—	6/-	5/3
Dunoon and Innellan	—	5/6	4/6
Rothesay and Wemyss Bay ...	—	5/-	3/9
Largs and Millport ...	—	3/9	3/9

To STRANRAER
Commences 9th June.
By Palatial Turbine Steamer "DUCHESS OF MONTROSE"
On THURSDAYS (weather permitting) (15th September excepted).
(Ceases after 22nd September.)

	a.m.		p.m.
Glasgow (St. Enoch) ......leave	7 30	Stranraer ....leave	2 0
Greenock (Princes Pier) ,,	8 35	eWhiting Bay ....arr.	5 15
Gourock ,,	8 45	bLamlash ,,	5 25
Dunoon ,,	9 0	aBrodick ,,	5 40
Innellan ,,	9 15	Millport (Keppel Pier) ,,	6 25
Craigmore ,,	9 50	Largs ,,	6 40
Rothesay ,,	9 45	Craigmore ,,	7 10
Largs ,,	10 15	Rothesay ,,	7 15
Millport (Keppel Pier) ,,	10 30	Innellan ,,	7 40
aBrodick ,,	11 15	Dunoon ,,	7 55
bLamlash ,,	11 25	Gourock ,,	8 15
eWhiting Bay ,,	11 30	Greenock (Princes Pier) ,,	8 30
Stranraer ....arr.	2 0p	Glasgow (St. Enoch) ,,	9 48

a Calls at Brodick on 9th and 30th June, 21st July, 11th August, and 1st and 22nd September.
b Calls at Lamlash on 16th June, 7th and 28th July, 18th August, and 8th September.
e Calls at Whiting Bay on 23rd June, 14th July, 4th and 25th August, and 15th September.

RETURN FARES.		
From	1st Class & Cabin.	3rd Class & Cabin.
Glasgow (St. Enoch)	9/6	8/-
Greenock, Gourock, Dunoon and Innellan ...	—	6/-
Craigmore, Rothesay, Largs and Millport ...	—	5/-
Brodick, Lamlash and Whiting Bay ...	—	4/-

The Tickets are valid on Day of Issue only.

Above left: On Tuesdays *Duchess of Montrose* sailed round the Islands of Arran and Ailsa Craig. On Saturday afternoons a trip round Ailsa Craig was offered, an excursion that survived until the end of her career.

Left: On Wednesdays *Duchess of Montrose* sailed to Ayr and on Thursdays until 1935 to Stranraer. From 1936 onwards she offered an Inveraray trip as a part replacement for *King George V*, now owned by MacBrayne.

Right: Duchess of Montrose also offered a selection of evening cruises, like this one in 1933 to Hermit's Isle (Holy Isle).

Below: A well-filled Duchess of Montrose, seen in 1934 in the Kyles of Bute.

SUNSET
—AT—
SEA
Over Arran's Purple Peaks.

PLEASANT SUNDAY EVENING SAIL
By World's Finest Turbine Steamer

'Duchess of Montrose'
—ON—

Sunday, 3rd September
—TO—

HERMIT'S ISLE,
Holy Isle, once the Home of St. Molio,
the Hermit Monk.
RETURNING OVER MOONLIT WATERS

Music by
SPECIAL ORCHESTRA
Relayed throughout the Ship by Loud Speakers.
COMMUNITY SINGING.

——Steamer Leaves——
Gourock 6.15; Dunoon 6.30; Rothesay 7.15;
Largs 7.45; Millport (Keppel Pier) 8 p.m.

The Promoter reserves the right to alter or cancel
this Cruise.
FARE 2/-

Haughey, Printer, Greenock.

77

Duchess of Montrose seen after the fitting of a full-size mainmast in 1934.

Duchess of Montrose approaching Wemyss Bay in wartime colours on 4 June 1945. At the end of September 1939 she was moved to Stranraer for the trooping service to Larne, but was within a short period replaced by *Duchess of Hamilton*, possibly because the latter had a bow rudder. In June and July 1940 she returned to the North Channel crossing to cope with heavy troop movements in the aftermath of Dunkirk. During the remainder of the war years she remained on the Clyde, sailing year-round on the Wemyss Bay to Rothesay run in the main, with a short spell on the Gourock to Dunoon service in January 1940 after *King Edward* was involved in a collision. In the winter months she fitted in an early afternoon trip to Largs and Keppel Pier, Cumbrae. (*Revd W.C. Galbraith, A. Ernest Glen Collection*)

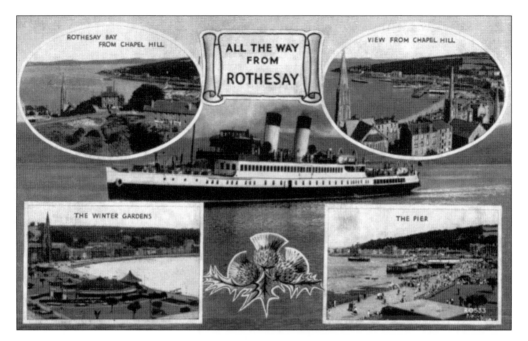

Duchess of Montrose returned to summer cruising duty in 1946 and, like the remainder of the fleet, received a wheelhouse in 1948. This was said to have been at the instigation of the National Union of Railwaymen, to whom the crews of the railway-owned Clyde steamers belonged. In the 1946-1947 winter she remained in service on railway connection work from Wemyss Bay to Innellan and Rothesay. In January 1948 she served Millport for five days. In April and May 1949 she was again on the Rothesay rail-connected sailings.

Duchess of Montrose departing from Dunoon. In the post-war years, she returned to the day excursion trade. In the summer of 1952 she mainly offered locally advertised sailings, but in 1953 returned to a cruise schedule. On Mondays, Thursdays and Saturdays she sailed for Lochranza and Campbeltown, on Tuesdays to Inveraray, on Wednesdays to Ayr, and on Fridays to Whiting Bay via the Kyles. From 1954 she sailed to Arran via the Kyles on Wednesdays and to Ayr on Fridays.

Left: Duchess of Montrose approaching Rothesay in her final years.

Below: A lightly-filled *Duchess of Montrose* in 1963.

Duchess of Montrose in Rothesay Bay.

Duchess of Montrose at Inveraray in 1963.

Above: Duchess of Montrose departing Campbeltown on a Monday in summer 1964, seen from *Caledonia*, which was on a Campbeltown day excursion from Ayr that day.

Left: Duchess of Montrose was withdrawn at the end of the 1964 season and is seen in Greenock's Albert Harbour in the 1964-1965 winter.

Duchess of Montrose in the Albert Harbour on the same occasion, with *Duchess of Hamilton* and *Queen Mary II* berthed alongside her. On 19 September 1965 she was towed away from the Clyde to the yard of Van Heyghen Fréres at Ghent for scrapping. *Queen Mary II* was already in the new 1965 colours.

Duchess of Hamilton in pre-war years, seen here on a trial run in a postcard from Adamson of Rothesay.

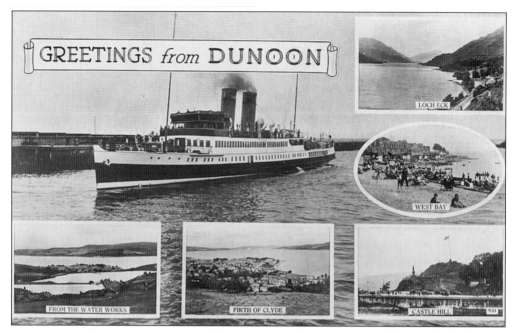

Duchess of Hamilton arriving at Ayr in a multi-view card with the title 'Greetings from Dunoon'. This card was used for various resorts with different inset views.

Duchess of Hamilton arriving at Rothesay dressed overall in mid-firth in pre-war years. She could be easily distinguished from her sister, e.g. in having four windows forward of the engine room opening whereas the *Montrose* had three, and also, later in her career, in having a crosstrees on her main mast.

Page 85, above left: The inaugural season's programme for *Duchess of Hamilton*, featuring a picture of *Duchess of Montrose*.

Above right: The cover of the 1939 Ayr excursion booklet. By now the photograph was correct and *Duchess of Hamilton* was a 'Palatial Turbine Steamer'.

London Midland and Scottish Railway Company and the Caledonian Steam Packet Company Ltd.

DAILY PLEASURE SAILINGS
BY NEW TURBINE STEAMER

DUCHESS OF HAMILTON

FROM AYR, TROON, ARDROSSAN, GIRVAN, MILLPORT, LARGS and ARRAN—Season 1932

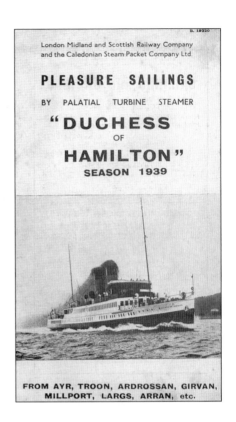

London Midland and Scottish Railway Company and the Caledonian Steam Packet Company Ltd.

PLEASURE SAILINGS
BY PALATIAL TURBINE STEAMER

"DUCHESS OF HAMILTON"
SEASON 1939

FROM AYR, TROON, ARDROSSAN, GIRVAN, MILLPORT, LARGS, ARRAN, etc.

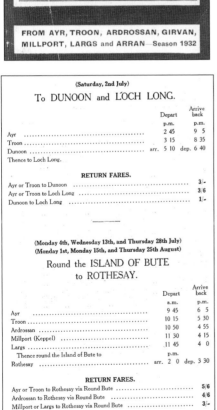

(Saturday, 2nd July)

To DUNOON and LOCH LONG.

	Depart	Arrive back
	p.m.	p.m.
Ayr	2 45	9 5
Troon	3 15	8 35
Dunoon	arr. 5 10	dep. 6 40
Thence to Loch Long.		

RETURN FARES.

Ayr or Troon to Dunoon	3/-
Ayr or Troon to Loch Long	3/6
Dunoon to Loch Long	1/-

(Monday 4th, Wednesday 13th, and Thursday 28th July)
(Monday 1st, Monday 15th, and Thursday 25th August)

Round the ISLAND OF BUTE to ROTHESAY.

	Depart	Arrive back
	a.m.	p.m.
Ayr	9 45	6 5
Troon	10 15	5 30
Ardrossan	10 50	4 55
Millport (Keppel)	11 30	4 15
Largs	11 45	4 0
Thence round the Island of Bute to		
Rothesay	arr. 2 0	dep. 3 30

RETURN FARES.

Ayr or Troon to Rothesay via Round Bute	5/6
Ardrossan to Rothesay via Round Bute	4/6
Millport or Largs to Rothesay via Round Bute	3/-

For Evening Cruises, see pages 23 and 24.

(Tuesdays, 5th and 26th July, and 2nd August)

To INVERARAY.
(LOCH FYNE)

	Depart	Arrive back
	a.m.	p.m.
Ayr	9 45	7 45
Whiting Bay	10 45	6 45
Lamlash	11 5	6 25
Brodick	11 30	6 0
Inveraray	arr. 2 15	dep. 3 15

RETURN FARES.

Ayr to Inveraray	5/6
Arran Piers to Inveraray	4/-

(Wednesday 6th July, Wednesday, 3rd and Tuesday 16th August)

To LOCHGOILHEAD
(Via DUNOON)

	Depart	Arrive back
	a.m.	p.m.
Ayr	9 45	6 40
Troon	10 15	6 10
Ardrossan	10 50	5 25
Millport (Keppel)	11 30	4 45
Largs	11 45	4 30
Dunoon	12 25	3 50
Lochgoilhead	arr. 1 20	dep. 2 50

RETURN FARES.

Ayr or Troon to Lochgoilhead	5/6
Ayr or Troon to Dunoon	4/6
Ayr or Troon to Millport or Largs	3/9
Ardrossan to Lochgoilhead	4/6
Ardrossan to Dunoon	3/9
Millport or Largs to Lochgoilhead	3/9
Millport or Largs to Dunoon	2/6
Dunoon to Lochgoilhead	2/7½

For Evening Cruises, see pages 23 and 24.

A Bus leaves Ayr Station at 9.15 a.m. Mondays to Fridays inclusive, for the Harbour in connection with the Sailings. Single fare 3d.

Timetables for the inaugural Ayr cruises of *Duchess of Hamilton* from 2 to 6 July 1932.

Sunday Cruises

from

AYR, TROON
and ARDROSSAN

By Palatial New Turbine Steamer
"DUCHESS OF HAMILTON"

or

Turbine Steamer "GLEN SANNOX"

Sunday, 3rd July	..	LOCHRANZA (Arran).
,, 10th July	..	*DUNOON AND LOCH GOIL.
,, 17th July	..	LOCH FYNE.
,, 24th July	..	ROUND THE ISLAND OF BUTE.
,, 31st July	..	*ROTHESAY AND LOCH STRIVEN.
,, 7th August	..	*DUNOON AND LOCH GOIL.
,, 14th August		LOCH FYNE.
,, 21st August	..	ROUND THE ISLAND OF BUTE.
,, 28th August	..	*ROTHESAY AND LOCH STRIVEN.
,, 4th September		LOCH FYNE.

* On Cruises to Dunoon and Loch Goil and Rothesay and Loch Striven, passengers may land at Dunoon or Rothesay respectively and rejoin steamer on return journey. Steamer arrives at Rothesay and Dunoon at 2.45 p.m. and returns at 4.15 p.m.

					Depart noon	Arrive back p.m.	Fare
AYR	..	..	..	..	12 0	6 50	4/-
TROON	..	..	..	..	12 30 p.m.	6 15	4/-
ARDROSSAN	..	..	..	..	1 10	5 40	3/-

Left: A series of Sunday cruises were featured by *Duchess of Hamilton* in her inaugural season.

Below: Duchess of Hamilton reversing out of Ayr Harbour in a pre-war postcard view.

Duchess of Hamilton served as a troopship on the Larne to Stranraer route from October 1939 to October 1940 and in 1945 and 1946. From 7 to 21 December 1941 she operated special milk runs from Larne to Stranraer. Between these periods she was used as a tender at Gourock, where she is seen here on 12 June 1945. (*Revd W.C. Galbraith, A. Ernest Glen Collection*)

On the evening of 26 December 1945 *Duchess of Hamilton* ran into an almost perpendicular cliff face just south of Corsewall Point, causing this damage to her bow. She managed to back off and to reach Stranraer under her own power.

Duchess of Hamilton arriving at Gourock on 2 July 1947. After the war she was used on day excursions from the upper Firth.

TIME-TABLE	AMUSEMENTS ON BOARD

TIME-TABLE

Outward

Leave Glasgow Bridge Wharf	9.00 a.m.
Leave Gourock Pier - - - -	11.00 a.m.
Arrive Ardrishaig - - - - -	2.00 p.m.

Inward

Leave Ardrishaig - - - - -	4.30 p.m.
Arrive Gourock - - - - - -	7.45 p.m.
„ Paisley (Gilmour St.) - -	8.33 p.m.
„ Glasgow (Central) - -	8.50 p.m.

Please see that ample time is allowed for returning to Steamer which must leave at 4.30 p.m. prompt.

CATERING ON STEAMER

LUNCH and TEA (Saloons & Tables as per tickets)

		Lunch	Tea
1st Sitting	-	11.00 a.m.	4.40 p.m.
2nd Sitting	-	11.45 a.m.	5.20 p.m.
3rd Sitting	-	12.30 p.m.	6.00 p.m.
4th Sitting	-	1.15 p.m.	6.40 p.m.

AMUSEMENTS ON BOARD

Pillow Fighting   Golf Bagatelle   Ninepins

Deck Quoits   Singing

Dancing

———

An Orchestra will play throughout the Cruise.

———

The course of Steamer will be set according to weather conditions.

———

At Ardrishaig

Bowling.   The Green will be available to members of the party.

Putting.   18-Hole Green on foreshore.

———

In the event of inclement weather the public hall adjacent to the Bowling Green will be open and an impromptu dance may be held.

Buses will meet the steamer and will be available for short tours at reasonable prices.

Parties wishing to arrange special tours should arrange their numbers beforehand and contact the bus office on arrival.

Duchess of Hamilton was used on charters for large organizations, e.g. this one for the South of Scotland Electricity Board Social and Recreation Associations from Glasgow Bridge Wharf to Ardrishaig on Saturday 1 June 1957. Note the on-board entertainment offered.

Duchess of Hamilton at Campbeltown in the early fifties. In the late fifties and early sixties she normally served Campbeltown five days a week, with a Wednesday trip to Arran via the Kyles and a Friday cruise to Ayr. On those days *Duchess of Montrose* served Campbeltown.

Duchess of Hamilton in the Kyles of Bute pre-1964.

Duchess of Hamilton in mid-Firth in 1964.

Duchess of Hamilton at Lamlash prior to 1955 when that pier was closed.

Duchess of Hamilton at Rothesay, taken from a self-drive motorboat in 1964.

A multiple-view postcard of *Duchess of Hamilton*, *Queen Mary II*, *Maid of Skelmorlie*, *Waverley* and *Glen Sannox*.

In 1965 *Duchess of Hamilton* received lions on her funnels and her hull was painted in what was named 'Monastral Blue' in common with the remainder of the CSP fleet. She is seen here at Lochranza.

Duchess of Hamilton made an unusual call at Girvan on 29 April 1967 on a Clyde River Steamer Club charter. The previous call by a Clyde steamer before that had been in the 1930s, although the port is now served regularly in the summer months by the paddle steamer *Waverley*.

Duchess of Hamilton leaving Rothesay Bay with Toward Lighthouse in the background, in a late sixties view.

Duchess of Hamilton at Campbeltown on 30 June 1968.

Duchess *of Hamilton* at Arrochar on a Clyde River Steamer Club charter on 7 September 1967.

In 1970, now under the Scottish Transport Group, the CSP hulls were painted black instead of the blue, which had been used for the previous five seasons. A smoky *Duchess of Hamilton* is seen here at Millport Keppel Pier on 5 September 1970 on another CRSC charter.

Duchess of Hamilton at Ardrishaig earlier on the same day.

Approaching Millport on *Duchess of Hamilton*.

In 1934, in keeping with the art deco designs of the age, two revolutionary-looking paddle steamers, *Mercury* and *Caledonia*, appeared in the fleet. Instead of conventional paddle boxes with radial or horizontal vents, they had concealed paddle boxes. It was said that they could thus be mistaken for turbine steamers from a distance. Both had three-crank triple expansion machinery. *Mercury* was the first to enter service. She was built by Fairfield's, entered service on 14 March, and is seen here leaving Kirn on 2 July of that year. *Mercury*, like the ex-GSWR paddler of the same name, was owned by the LMSR until 1937 when, along with *Glen Rosa*, the last surviving ex-GSWR steamer, she was transferred to the CSP.

Mercury at Greenock Princes Pier, with a Cunard liner in the background, at the Tail of the Bank. Her normal route was from Princess Pier via Gourock, Dunoon, Rothesay and intermediate piers to the Kyles of Bute.

To the KYLES OF BUTE and ORMIDALE (Loch Ridden)

By Palatial Steamers "Mercury" and "Caledonia"
(OR OTHER STEAMER)

OUTWARD.		Daily. a.m.	Sats. only. p.m.	INWARD.		Daily. p.m.	Sats. only. p.m.
Glasgow { St. Enoch .... dep.		9 20	1 43	Ormidale .... dep.		12 50	5 40
Glasgow { Central .... ,,		9 50	2 0	Auchenlochan .... ,,		1 45	5 15
Paisley (Gilmour Street) .. ,,		10 2	1 57	Tighnabruaich .... ,,		1 50	5 22
Greenock (Princes Pier) .. ,,		10 25	2 30	Colintraive .... ,,		2 5	5 55
Gourock .... ,,		10 48	2 50	Port Bannatyne .... arr.		2 30	6 20
Kirn .... ,,		11 5	3 5	Rothesay .... ,,		2 45	6 30
Dunoon .... ,,		11 10	3 10	Craigmore .... ,,		3 0	6 45
Innellan .... ,,		11 30	3 30	Innellan .... ,,		3 20	7 5
Craigmore .... ,,		11 50	3 50	Dunoon .... ,,		3 40	7 25
Rothesay .... ,,		12 0n	4 0	Kirn .... ,,		3 45	7 30
Port Bannatyne .... ,,		12 10p	—	Gourock .... ,,		4 5	7 50
Colintraive .... arr.		12 35	4 35	Greenock (Princes Pier) .. ,,		4 20	8 5
Tighnabruaich .... ,,		1 10	4 50	Paisley (Gilmour Street) .. ,,		4b53	8b27
Auchenlochan .... ,,		1 15	4 55	Glasgow { Central .... ,,		5 10	8 33
Ormidale .... ,,		12 50	5 40	Glasgow { St. Enoch .... ,,		5d26	9 0

b Via Gourock.   *d* Arrives at 5.12 p.m. on Saturdays.

RETURN FARES.

FROM	Day Excursion. Applying on Forenoon Steamer.			Saturday Afternoon Excursion.		
	1st Class and Saloon	3rd Class and Saloon	3rd Class Rail and Steamer	1st Class and Saloon	3rd Class and Saloon	3rd Class Rail and Steamer
	s. d.	s. d.	s. d.	s. d.	s. d.	s. d.
Glasgow and Paisley	6 9	5 6	4 6	6 9	5 6	4 6
Greenock and Gourock	—	3 9	3 0	—	2 6	—
Kirn, Dunoon and Innellan	—	3 0	2 3	—	2 0	—
Craigmore, Rothesay or Port-Bannatyne	—	1 6	1 0	—	1 0	—

A summer 1935 timetable for the above route to the Kyles of Bute.

96

Mercury departing from Rothesay, with *Queen Mary II* and *Marmion* at the pier.

Before the days of the car ferry, cars were loaded onto paddle steamers by means of two planks at a convenient state of the tide. A car is here being loaded on to *Mercury* at Millport. *Mercury* was called up for minesweeping in 1939 and was based firstly at Portland and later at Milford Haven. She sank while under tow after one of her own mines became trapped in her own gear and exploded on Christmas Day 1940, blowing her stern off. *Caledonia* (HMS *Goatfell* at the time) tried to save her but was unsuccessful.

ATTRACTIVE AFTERNOON CRUISES

By Palatial Steamer "CALEDONIA"

DAILY except SATURDAYS.

DAILY except SATURDAYS—TO LARGS AND MILLPORT (31st July and 1st August excepted).

			AFTERNOON RETURN FARES.
From	Rothesay ..	a12.0 noon	}
"	Craigmore ..	a12.5 p.m.	.. .. 1/-

Returning from Millport at a1.15, 3.0, c4.20, and A5.30 p.m., Largs 1.50, 2.30, c4.45, and A5.5 p.m.

MONDAYS and WEDNESDAYS—TO LOCH LONG (5th and 10th June and 10th and 31st July excepted).

From	Millport (Old Pier)	1.15 p.m.	}	
"	Largs	1.50 p.m.	} Millport or Largs to Loch Long	1/3
"	Rothesay ..	2.30 p.m.	} Rothesay and Craigmore to Loch Long	
"	Craigmore ..	2.35 p.m.	}	1/-

Arriving back at Rothesay 4.20, Craigmore 4.35, Largs 5.0, Millport 5.30 p.m.

MONDAYS and WEDNESDAYS—TO LARGS AND MILLPORT (5th and 10th June and 10th and 31st July excepted).

From	Dunoon ..	3.40 p.m.	..	Dunoon to Largs or Millport	..	..	1/6
"	Rothesay ..	4.30 p.m.	}	Rothesay or Craigmore to Largs or Millport			
"	Craigmore ..	4.35 p.m.	}				1/-

Arriving back at Rothesay 6.15 p.m., Craigmore 6.35 p.m., Dunoon 7.10 p.m.

TUESDAYS and THURSDAYS—TO DUNOON AND ROTHESAY (1st August excepted).

From	Millport (Old Pier)	1.15 p.m.	}	
"	Largs	1.50 p.m.	} Millport or Largs to Dunoon and Rothesay	1/3
"	Dunoon ..	2.35 p.m.	} Dunoon to Rothesay	1/-

Returning from Rothesay at 3.35 p.m. and arriving back at Dunoon 4.15 p.m., Largs 5.0 p.m., Millport 5.30 p.m.

Passengers may return from Rothesay at 4.25 p.m. or c4.50 p.m. for Largs and Millport and at 4.35 p.m. or 6.30 p.m. to Dunoon.

TUESDAYS and THURSDAYS—TO LARGS AND MILLPORT (1st August excepted).

From	Rothesay ..	3.35 p.m.	}	Rothesay or Craigmore to Largs or Millport	1/3
"	Craigmore ..	3.40 p.m.	}	Dunoon to Largs or Millport	1/6
"	Dunoon ..	4.15 p.m.	}	Rothesay or Craigmore to Dunoon	1/-

Arriving back at Rothesay 6.15, Craigmore 6.35, Dunoon 7.10.

Passengers from Rothesay may land at Dunoon and return by L.N.E.R. Steamer at 5.10 or 6.30 p.m. and by L.M.S. Steamer at 8.5 p.m.

FRIDAYS—TO KYLES OF BUTE AND LOCH RIDDEN (also Wed. 5th, Mon. 10th June, and Wed. 10th July).

From	Millport (Old Pier)	a1.15 p.m.	}	
"	Largs	1.50 p.m.	} Millport or Largs to Kyles of Bute	1/3
"	Craigmore ..	2.20 p.m.	}	
"	Rothesay ..	2.30 p.m.	} Rothesay, Craigmore or Port-Bannatyne	
"	Port-Bannatyne ..	2.40 p.m.	} to Kyles of Bute	1/-

Arriving back at Port-Bannatyne 4.10, Rothesay 4.20, Craigmore 4.35, Largs d5.0, Millport d5.30.

FRIDAYS—TO LARGS AND MILLPORT (also Wed. 5th, Mon. 10th June and Wed. 10th July).

| From | Rothesay .. | h4.30 p.m. | } | |
| " | Craigmore .. | 4.35 p.m. | } .. .. 1/- |

Arriving back at Rothesay 6.15, Craigmore 6.35 p.m.

---

a Does not call at Millport on 5th and 10th June and 10th July.
b 4.25 p.m. on 5th and 10th June and 10th July.
c Via Wemyss Bay.
d On 5th and 10th June and 10th July arrive back Millport 5.10, Largs 5.25 p.m.
f 5th and 10th June and 10th July excepted.
h On 5th and 10th June and 10th July leave Millport 5.10, Largs 5.35 p.m.

Above: The second new steamer of 1934 was *Caledonia*. She was a sister of *Mercury*, but was built at the yard of William Denny & Bros Ltd at Dumbarton, the first Clyde paddle steamer to come from there since *Duchess of Hamilton* in 1890, and is seen here on trials.

Left: Caledonia was initially placed on railway connection work from Wemyss Bay and on a series of afternoon excursions, as this extract from the 1935 summer timetable shows.

An empty *Caledonia* on a trial trip off Gourock in her early years.

A postcard view of *Caledonia* taken in 1935 at Rothesay with *King Edward* and *Waverley*. In the summer seasons of 1936 to 1938 *Caledonia* served on the Arran via the Kyles day excursion, replacing *Duchess of Argyll*, and in 1939 alternated with *Mercury* between this sailing and a Rothesay-based Kyles and railway connection roster.

Caledonia served during the war as the minesweeper HMS *Goatfell*, and was later used as a patrol vessel. She took part in the D-Day landings in Normandy and in the relief of Antwerp.

Caledonia returned to the Clyde in 1946 on the Wemyss Bay to Rothesay service. From 1954 she was used as the Ayr excursion steamer, and is seen here arriving at Campbeltown in that period. The Ayr excursion steamer made a regular weekly visit to Campbeltown in that era.

Caledonia arriving at Millport (Old Pier) on winter service.

A postcard view of a well-filled *Caledonia* in that era. In 1948, in common with the remainder of the fleet, she received a wheelhouse.

Caledonia arriving at Dunoon in the early sixties.

In 1965, *Caledonia* received lions on her funnel and a Monastral Blue hull in common with the remainder of the fleet. She was transferred from Ayr to Craigendoran to provide a replacement for the now withdrawn *Jeanie Deans*, and provided a variety of excursions from there, including Round Bute, to Arrochar, Round the Lochs, and to Arran via the Kyles. She is seen here at Rothesay.

Caledonia at Craigendoran on 4 May 1968 on a Clyde River Steamer Club charter to Ardrishaig and Inveraray.

Caledonia at Ardrishaig on the same day.

Caledonia at Inveraray later in the same day.

The destination board for that cruise, which continued up Loch Fyne to Dunderave Castle.

Caledonia arriving at Gourock with an Ellerman City liner departing in the background.

Caledonia dressed overall at Campbeltown, also on a CRSC charter, this time on 13 September 1969, her last charter by the CRSC.

Opposite top: In 1969 *Caledonia* spent ten days in April on charter to David MacBrayne Ltd, and a spell at the beginning of October on the Tarbert mail service. From 1 October, the CSP took over the mail service to Tarbert. The latter occasion was, in fact, her last week in service after which she was withdrawn.

Caledonia alongside *Waverley* in winter lay-up in Rothesay Dock in the 1969-1970 winter.

In early 1970, *Caledonia* was sold to the shipbreakers Arnott Young & Co., and moved to their yard in Dalmuir basin, where she is seen here. They renamed her *Old Caledonia*. A campaign to save her was mounted successfully by the Scottish branch of the Paddle Steamer Preservation Society.

Old Caledonia was purchased by brewers Bass Charrington, and towed to the Thames where she was used as a floating pub near Waterloo Bridge.

On 27 April 1980, *Old Caledonia* was gutted by fire, and was later broken up at Grays in Essex. Her engines were saved and are now on exhibit at the Hollycombe Steam Collection near Liphook in Hampshire, where they are occasionally steamed, using steam from the boiler for a steam sawmill.

In 1935 *Marchioness of Lorne*, a smaller version of *Mercury* and *Caledonia* was built by Fairfield. She again had triple expansion machinery and was designed to replace *Marchioness of Breadalbane* on the Holy Loch run. *Marchioness of Lorne* remained in service on the Clyde during the war, and is seen here leaving Hunters Quay on 22 June 1940.

Marchioness of Lorne in 1947. She remained on the Holy Loch run until 1952.

Marchioness of Lorne at Gourock in 1952. In 1953 she was moved to the Wemyss Bay to Millport service, but was not liked there because she was too slow. To replace her *Talisman* was re-engined and moved to the Millport run. The *Lorne* was replaced by *Talisman* in June 1954 and laid up in the Albert harbour until sold for scrapping at Port Glasgow in February 1955.

Above: Wee Cumbrae was a small motorboat built in 1935 by Denny for a new Largs to Millport service. She was built to compete with the privately owned *Cramond Brig*, which had started running on the route the previous summer.

Right: Wee Cumbrae approaching Millport. She was used during the war as an examination vessel based at Rothesay and, in 1947, had a spell on the Gourock to Dunoon service. She was sold in March 1953, and left the Clyde as deck cargo on a cargo ship for a new owner in Brunei. (*A. Ernest Glen Collection*)

Another turbine steamer appeared in 1936, *Marchioness of Graham*. She was built, again, by Fairfield, and is seen here on trials on 7 April of that year. She replaced the ex-GSWR turbine *Atalanta* on the Ardrossan to Arran route and enabled *Glen Sannox* to commence a Campbeltown service. She also offered Sunday cruises from Gourock.

Marchioness of Graham in a Leo Vogt photograph, with the Campbeltown steamer *Dalriada* at Wemyss Bay on 1 January 1940. She mainly undertook the sailings from Wemyss Bay and Largs to Millport and, in the summer months, Kilchattan Bay, during the war years.

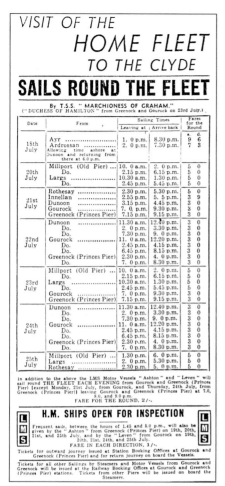
Above: From 1947 to 1953 *Marchioness of Graham* undertook the Ayr excursion service. This sheet gives details of sailings from 20 to 31 August 1947. She was also the winter Arran steamer in this period.

Above left: Marchioness of Graham undertook a series of sailings for a Royal Naval fleet review in July 1947.

Marchioness of Graham leaving Troon in the early fifties.

THE PIER AND HARBOUR, CAMPBELTOWN, ARGYLL   B 3086

Marchioness of Graham half-hidden behind the pier sheds at Campbeltown along with *Duchess of Hamilton*.

In 1954, with the withdrawal of *Glen Sannox*, *Marchioness of Graham* became the year-round Arran steamer, and is seen here in that year in Brodick Bay. She remained coal-fired and was withdrawn after the 1957 season, being sold to Nicholas Diapoulis of Greece in January 1959. Note the car on deck at the foot of the funnel.

The *Marchioness of Graham* was extensively rebuilt in Greece, including the addition of cabin accommodation, and was renamed *Hellas*. In 1963 she was renamed *Nea Hellas*, in 1964, *Galaxias*, and again in 1966, *El Greco*. She was laid up after the 1967 season and was broken up in 1975. (*Richard Orr*)

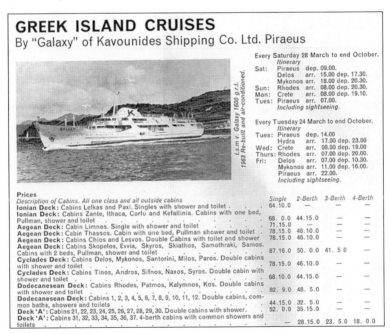

GREEK ISLAND CRUISES
By "Galaxy" of Kavounides Shipping Co. Ltd. Piraeus

t.s.m.v. Galaxy 1600 g.r.t.
1963 Re-built and air-conditioned.

Every Saturday 28 March to end October.
Itinerary

Sat:	Piraeus	dep. 09.00.	
	Delos	arr. 15.00 dep. 17.30.	
	Mykonos	arr. 18.00 dep. 20.30.	
Sun:	Rhodes	arr. 08.00 dep. 20.30.	
Mon:	Crete	arr. 08.00 dep. 19.10.	
Tues:	Piraeus	arr. 07.00.	
	Including sightseeing.		

Every Tuesday 24 March to end October.
Itinerary

Tues:	Piraeus	dep. 14.00	
	Hydra	arr. 17.00 dep. 23.00	
Wed:	Crete	arr. 08.00 dep. 19.00	
Thurs:	Rhodes	arr. 07.00 dep. 20.00.	
Fri:	Delos	arr. 07.00 dep. 10.30.	
	Mykonos	arr. 11.00 dep. 16.00.	
	Piraeus	arr. 22.00.	
	Including sightseeing.		

Prices
Description of Cabins. All one class and all outside cabins

	Single	2-Berth	3-Berth	4-Berth
Ionian Deck: Cabins Lefkas and Paxi. Singles with shower and toilet .	64.10.0	—	—	—
Ionian Deck: Cabins Zante, Ithaca, Corfu and Kefallinia. Cabins with one bed, Pullman, shower and toilet	68. 0.0	44.15.0	—	—
Aegean Deck: Cabin Limnos. Single with shower and toilet .	71.15.0	—	—	—
Aegean Deck: Cabin Thassos. Cabin with one bed, Pullman shower and toilet .	78.15.0	46.10.0	—	—
Aegean Deck: Cabins Chios and Lesvos. Double Cabins with toilet and shower .	78.15.0	46.10.0	—	—
Aegean Deck: Cabins Skopelos, Evvia, Skyros, Skiathos, Samothraki, Samos. Cabins with 2 beds, Pullman, shower and toilet .	87.16.0	50. 0.0	41. 5 0	—
Cyclades Deck: Cabins Delos, Mykonos, Santorini, Milos, Paros. Double cabins with shower and toilet .	78.15.0	46.10.0	—	—
Cyclades Deck: Cabins Tinos, Andros, Sifnos, Naxos, Syros. Double cabin with shower and toilet .	68.10.0	44.15.0	—	—
Dodecanesean Deck: Cabins Rhodes, Patmos, Kalymnos, Kos. Double cabins with shower and toilet .	82. 9.0	48. 5.0	—	—
Dodecanesean Deck: Cabins 1, 2, 3, 4, 5, 6, 7, 8, 9, 10, 11, 12. Double cabins, common baths, showers and toilets .	44.15.0	32. 5.0	—	—
Deck 'A': Cabins 21, 22, 23, 24, 25, 26, 27, 28, 29, 30. Double cabins with shower.	52. 0.0	35.15.0	—	—
Deck 'A': Cabins 31, 32, 33, 34, 35, 36, 37. 4-berth cabins with common showers and toilets .	—	28.15.0	23. 5.0	18. 0.0

An extract from a 1964 Greek holiday brochure featuring cruises by *Galaxy* (an anglicized form of *Galaxias*) showing fares for an amazing variety of cabin accommodation. By this time she was sailing under charter to Kavounides Shipping Co. Ltd., and sailing on Aegean passenger service from Piraeus to Tinos and Mykonos in the winter months as *Andros II*.

In 1936 a new Post Office mail contract for Arran commenced which required the mail to be in Brodick by 0800. The CSP responded by building the coaster *Arran Mail* for this service. A product of the Denny yard, she entered service in July of that year and made one daily crossing, leaving Ardrossan at 0645 with mail and newspapers. She had a passenger certificate for ten passengers. The service was withdrawn a few days after the outbreak of war and she acted as a tender to ships at the Tail of the Bank during the war years.

Arran Mail resumed the Arran mail service after 1945, but by November 1949 the cargo to Arran had become too much for her and she was withdrawn. In December 1951 she was sold to Gibraltan owners. She was later renamed *Saint Ernest* and owned in Alderney. On 19 January 1962 she sank en route from Alderney to Newport with a cargo of broccoli. Her crew of five were lost.

Two more concealed paddle-box paddle steamers joined the fleet in 1937, *Jupiter* and *Juno*, built by Fairfield. Space for carrying cars was provided between the two funnels. Both had triple expansion machinery. *Jupiter* was the first to enter service, on 2 June 1937, and operated the Kyles and Rothesay services in that summer. She is seen here in pre-war condition.

Jupiter saw war service as the minesweeper HMS *Scawfell*. She was based at Ardrossan, then Portsmouth, was on the Clyde again, and then at Milford Haven. In 1941 she was converted to an auxiliary anti-aircraft ship based on the East Coast of England. She shot down three enemy aircraft and also had three 'probables'. In June 1944 she was involved in the D-Day landings, and was then stationed off the Isle of Wight to combat the V1 missiles, later running as a supply ship from the Thames to Antwerp. She returned to service on the Clyde in February 1946.

Top: Jupiter returned to the Gourock to Rothesay and the Kyles route after the war, and is seen here in Rothesay Bay.

Middle: Jupiter as a tender to a Cunard liner, flying the Cunard house-flag on her mainmast.

Bottom: In 1956 and 1957 *Jupiter* operated a summer service from Glasgow (Bridge Wharf) to Lochgoilhead, where she is seen here. At the end of the 1957 season she was withdrawn and lay in the Albert Harbour until sold for scrapping at Dublin in April 1961. Plans for further service operating out of Bournemouth came to nothing.

Juno, the last paddle steamer to be built for the Caledonian Steam Packet Co., entered service on 3 July 1937. She served, like her sister, on the Greenock Princes Pier to Rothesay and the Kyles services.

Juno at Dunoon Pier with *King Edward* approaching and *Marchioness of Lorne* in the distance, to the right of *Juno's* fore funnel.

Juno at Wemyss Bay, with *Duchess of Fife* behind the pier. Like her sister, she was called up as a minesweeper, being named HMS *Helvellyn*. On the night of 19 March 1941, while berthed in the Surrey Commercial Docks in London, she was hit by a bomb between the funnels and sank.

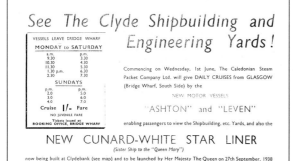

See The Clyde Shipbuilding and Engineering Yards!

VESSELS LEAVE BRIDGE WHARF
MONDAY to SATURDAY

a.m.	p.m.
9.30	3.30
10.30	4.30
11.30	5.30
1.30 p.m.	6.30
2.30	7.30

SUNDAYS

p.m.	p.m.
2.0	5.0
3.0	6.0
4.0	7.0

Cruise 1/- Fare
NO JUVENILE FARE
Tickets issued at
BOOKING OFFICE, BRIDGE WHARF

Commencing on Wednesday, 1st June, The Caledonian Steam Packet Company Ltd. will give DAILY CRUISES from GLASGOW (Bridge Wharf, South Side) by the

NEW MOTOR VESSELS

"ASHTON" and "LEVEN"

enabling passengers to view the Shipbuilding, etc. Yards, and also the

NEW CUNARD-WHITE STAR LINER
(Sister Ship to the "Queen Mary")

now being built at Clydebank (see map) and to be launched by Her Majesty The Queen on 27th September, 1938

Left: In 1938 the Empire Exhibition was being held in Glasgow and two small launches were built to run a service on the River Clyde to see the new Cunard White Star liner, which would become *Queen Elizabeth*, being built.

Ashton and *Leven* were both built by Denny of Dumbarton, and in their first season, 1938, sported white hulls. *Leven* is seen here in the river at Glasgow off Bridge Wharf.

In 1939 the hulls were repainted black, but the river service continued. Both were used during the war as tenders and in 1946 were placed on the Gourock to Dunoon service. In 1952 they operated a service to Kilcreggan and Blairmore. *Leven* is seen here approaching Gourock.

From 1952 until 1964 *Ashton* and *Leven* operated the Largs to Millport ferry service. *Ashton* is seen here arriving at Millport.

On 12 October 1962, *Ashton* had a two-day charter for Glasgow University Railway Society from Bowling to Kirkintilloch along the Forth and Clyde Canal, which was shortly to close to shipping.

Above right: Ashton was sold in 1965 to Walter Ritchie of Gourock and renamed *Gourockian* for the Gourock to Helensburgh service. In 1971 she was sold to Fleetwood and renamed *Wyre Lady* for the Fleetwood to Knott End ferry service. In 1976 she was sold for use on the River Severn at Holt Fleet and again the following year to Alan Oliver (Cruises) Ltd of Sprotsborough, near Doncaster, where she remains, operating on the Sheffield and South Yorkshire Navigation from Rotherham, Mexborough, Sprotsborough and Doncaster, with a Sunday waterbus service from Sprotsborough to Doncaster and Conisburgh. She is seen here at Fleetwood.

Above left: Leven was sold in 1965 to an owner at Larne, Northern Ireland, and almost immediately to the South Western Steam Navigation Co. of Paignton, Devon. They renamed her *Pride of the Bay*. She operated in the Torbay area and was later sold for use at Jersey, where she operated short coastal cruises, as advertised in this leaflet.

Above: In 2001 *Pride of the Bay* was sold to a Bristol Channel owner and now, named *Bristol Queen*, she offers cruises from Weston-Super-Mare to Steep Holm. She is seen here laid up at Bristol in late 2001 alongside *Balmoral*. *Balmoral* is sporting a temporary livery for a charter to BBC Scotland where she took the guise of MacBrayne's *Clydesdale* for a Gaelic TV serial.

Right: In 1939 the CSP considered various designs by Ferguson Bros of Port Glasgow for a car ferry for the Gourock to Dunoon route. Design 1a (top) was for an engines-aft motorship with a nineteen-car capacity and the type of hoist loading later seen in the ABC car ferries. Design 1b (centre) was similar, but with the engines exhausted through narrow pipes and a dummy funnel in the conventional position. Design 2 (bottom) had no hoist but access to the car deck by sliding doors.

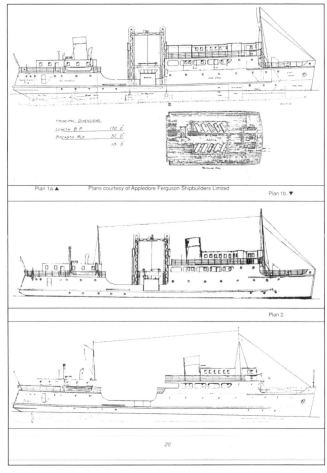

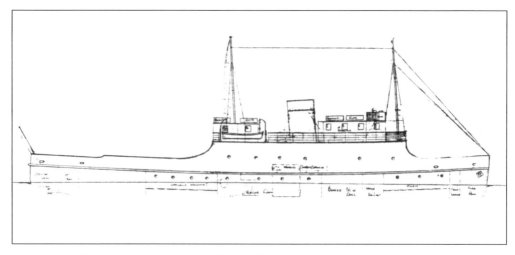

Design 3 was for a steam-powered vessel, possibly with reciprocating engines and a capacity for twenty-eight cars, but with less passenger accommodation. With the outbreak of war, none of these designs was proceeded with. It was to be a further fifteen years before a car ferry appeared on the Firth.

In 1938 the dredger *Carrick* was built for use at the Ayrshire ports and also at Wemyss Bay by the LMS. She was built by Wm Simons Ltd at Renfrew to succeed the dredger *Kyle*, which had been inherited with the GSWR fleet and remained in service until 1968, when she was sold to Sicilian owners and broken up in 1984. She is seen here at Ayr on 20 January 1949. (*James Currie*)

Four
Nationalised
1948-1972

Denny of Dumbarton had built *Countess of Breadalbane* for the CSP in 1936 for service on Loch Awe. She offered a service from Loch Awe station to Ford at the south end of the loch, where she is seen here, and also, in post-war years, short cruises at the head of the loch.

Top: In 1952 *Countess of Breadalbane* was moved from Loch Awe to the Clyde. Here she is seen being manoeuvred across the Callander & Oban Railway line near Loch Awe station.

Middle: After being hauled to Inveraray by road, *Countess of Breadalbane* tasted salt water for the first time, and is seen here alongside *The Second Snark*, Denny's tender.

Bottom: Before entering service on the Clyde, *Countess of Breadalbane* had her lower saloon windows replaced by portholes. While on the Clyde she offered short cruises and, in the 1952-1953 winter, covered the Holy Loch service. She also offered a connection from Rothesay to Tighnabruaich on Friday evenings in the summer and morning sailings from Innellan to Wemyss Bay. In the early sixties she sailed with a white hull, which, as seen here, tended to easily become rust-streaked.

Countess of Breadalbane at Ormidale on a Clyde River Steamer Club charter on 30 May 1964. Other CRSC charters had taken her to Paisley in 1959, Loch Striven in 1960, Millport in 1961, Glasgow Bridge Wharf on a Comet 150th Anniversary cruise in 1962 and to Carrick Castle and Lochgoilhead in 1963. In 1965 she made a ferry landing at Ardentinny, in 1966 she called at Kames, in 1967 at Arrochar, in 1969 Carrick Castle again, and in 1970 did a round of the smaller piers as a farewell cruise.

Countess of Breadalbane on an unusual winter charter, taking Santa Claus up-river to Lewis's department store in Glasgow Argyle Street.

Top: In 1965, with the withdrawal of *Ashton* and *Leven*, *Countess of Breadalbane*, now with a Monastral Blue hull, moved to the Largs to Millport service.

Middle: *Countess of Breadalbane* at the inner berth at Millport (Old) Pier. In 1967, replaced by *Keppel*, she took up the Holy Loch service.

Bottom: *Countess of Breadalbane* was withdrawn in May 1971. In November of that year she was sold to W.Roy Ritchie of Gourock and replaced *Gourockian*, ex-*Ashton*, in his fleet. In March 1972 she commenced a service to Blairmore initially as *Countess* and later as *Countess of Kempock*. This lasted not much more than a year, and she was then placed on the Gourock to Helensburgh service. She is seen here in the River Clyde, standing in for *Queen of Scots*, as *Countess of Kempock*.

126

On 30 December 1978, the Paddle Steamer Preservation Society chartered *Countess of Kempock* for their very first Christmas cruise to Carrick Castle, seen here, which took place in a blizzard.

On 18 October 1978, Roy Ritchie died and his widow did not carry on the business. In March 1979 *Countess of Kempock* was purchased by Offshore Workboats Ltd and, for the 1979 and 1980 summers was chartered to Staffa Marine to provide a service from Ulva Ferry on Mull to Staffa and Iona, at both of which she landed passengers, at Staffa by tender, and at Iona by berthing at the jetty there at high tide, otherwise being tendered. In 1981 Offshore Workboats Ltd operated her on cruises out of Oban. She is seen here in the Sound of Mull. She sailed twice a week to Tobermory, and three days a week for Craignure. In 1982 cruises from Eastbourne and Hastings were advertised but never took place.

The paddle steamer *Maid of the Loch*, on Loch Lomond, had been withdrawn at the end of the 1981 season. Ind Coope Alloa Brewery purchased her in March 1982 and, at the same time, purchased *Countess of Kempock*. She was moved by road to Balloch on 29 April 1982, having been sliced in two horizontally, and was reassembled at Balloch. She was named *Countess Fiona*, fitted with a dummy funnel, and entered service on the loch on 24 May 1982. She sailed in a similar schedule to *Maid of the Loch*, with calls at Luss, Rowardennan, and Inversnaid. She is seen here alongside a laid-up *Maid of the Loch* at Balloch Pier in October 1982.

For the 1989 season, *Countess Fiona* was rebuilt with a full-width saloon and a smaller motorship-type funnel, She is seen here arriving at Luss in that summer when she was under the joint ownership of James Fisher & Sons of Barrow in Furness and the Sea Management Corporation of Australia.

An upper decks shot of *Countess Fiona* in the 1989 season. This was to prove her final season in service, and she languished on the slipway at Balloch for a further ten years, gradually becoming more vandalized, until broken up by a bulldozer in late summer 1999.

In 1953-1954, the CSP took delivery of seven new motor vessels, four mid-size passenger ships of the Maid class, and three hoist-loading car ferries of the ABC class. *Maid of Ashton* was the first of these to be launched, on 17 February 1953. She was built, uniquely for a Clyde steamer, at Yarrow's yard at Scotstoun. *Maid of Ashton* spent much of her Clyde career on the Holy Loch service, from Gourock to Kilcreggan, Blairmore, and Kilmun. Calls at Cove, Strone, and Ardnadam had ceased during or shortly after the war. She is seen here arriving at Gourock in 1962.

Left: An empty *Maid of Ashton* at Rothesay Pier.

Below: A stern view of *Maid of Ashton*, which had just left Rothesay.

Bottom: Maid of Ashton with her forward saloon windows winter-boarded at Gourock Pier, with *Maid of Skelmorlie* aft of her at the mooring known as 'the wires'.

Passengers disembarking from *Maid of Ashton* at Ardrishaig in spring 1969. The metal plates that were fitted over the forward saloon windows, known historically as 'winter boarding' can be seen in detail here. She was withdrawn and laid up in 1971.

In 1972 *Maid of Ashton* was sold to an owner on the Thames and, after alteration, was berthed in central London as a private dining club, initially named *Hispaniola II*, and later *Hispaniola*. In more recent years she has become a public restaurant and, since this photograph was taken, has been moved down river east of Hungerford Bridge to a position near *Queen Mary*. In spring 2002 she was purchased by City Cruises from her previous owners, the Yardarm Club. She was towed to the George Prior yard at Ipswich for hull inspection and a refit.

M.V. Maid of Argyll.   CRS.5

Above: Maid of Argyll was the second Maid to appear. She was launched on 4 March 1953 at the yard of A&J Inglis at Pointhouse. She mainly operated on the Craigendoran and Gourock to Dunoon, Innellan and Rothesay service, and the Saturday Arrochar service, when *Waverley* was put on rail-connected services for the hordes of holidaymakers travelling to the main resorts of Dunoon and Rothesay and starting and finishing their holidays on a Saturday.

On 17 September 1966, *Maid of Argyll* made a special sailing up the River Cart, on another Clyde River Steamer Club charter from Paisley to Dunoon and Loch Striven. Following this the River Cart, from the Babcock & Wilcox works at Renfrew upstream to Paisley, was closed to navigation.

Maid of Argyll at Rothesay in 1969.

Maid of Argyll was the only one of the four Maids to survive in original condition to carry the new CalMac livery in 1973, and is seen here in Greenock's East India Harbour in spring of that year, alongside *Duchess of Hamilton*, which had had an extra fixture welded to her aft deck for an abortive attempt at using her in a static role at Glasgow under the ownership of Reo Stakis.

Maid of Argyll was sold at the end of 1973 to a company trading as Cycladic Cruises of Piraeus, and commenced a new career sailing from Flisvos marina, at Palaeon Phaleron, east of the main port of Piraeus, on day cruises to the Saronic Islands of Aegina, Poros and Hydra. In her first season, her landing platform was extended to form a small upper deck. By 1978, the upper deck was extended almost to the stern, and fitted out as a sun deck. By that time, she had been superseded in the service by *City of Hydra*, ex-*Claymore*, and saw little service, mainly sailing as a relief ship and on charters.Around 1989, *City of Piraeus* moved to Corfu and commenced day excursion sailings from there for Aronis Coastal Cruises as *City of Corfu*. These sailed to the island of Paxos and Parga on the mainland. She is seen here approaching Paxos on 21 July 1994. In 1997 she was seriously damaged by fire and, as far as is known, did not sail again. (*Ian Hall*)

Opposite, middle: Maid of Skelmorlie leaving Rothesay in autumn 1972, towards the close of her Clyde career. She was sold in April 1973 and renamed *Ala*.

Opposite, bottom: Ala was converted to become a small car ferry, with space for a limited number of cars aft, and in early 1976 she entered service in the Bay of Naples, owned by Giuffre & Lauro, sailing from Sorrento to Capri. She is seen here leaving the latter port.

Right: The third Maid to be launched, on 2 April 1953, also from A&J Inglis, was *Maid of Skelmorlie.* She mainly sailed from Wemyss Bay to Largs and Millport, although some sailings were extended to Rothesay to provide a 'Cumbrae Circle' cruise. She is seen here at Gourock, in January 1970 while on the Tarbert mail service, which she operated in the 1969-1970 winter. Note the shelter that had been fitted aft for parcels and luggage.

The former Maid made the Sorrento to Capri service her own for twenty years until laid up after the 1995 season. From 1997 to 1999 she was chartered to Adriatica for a winter cargo service to the Tremiti Islands in the Adriatic, and in summer 2001 was chartered to Di Maio for a route from Pozzuoli, north of Naples, to the island of Procida and is seen here at Pozzuoli on 12 August of that year. (*Arturo Lauriano, courtesy of Admeto Verde*)

Maid of Cumbrae, seen here in a postcard view at Largs, was the fourth and final Maid to be launched, on 13 May 1953 from Ardrossan Dockyard Ltd. This was another builder which had not previously built a Clyde Steamer. She could be distinguished from the other three by having her name on the dark portion of the hull, rather than the white upper strake. She performed a variety of short cruises, including forenoon café cruises, with a free cup of coffee and chocolate biscuit included, and afternoon cruises to such places as Dunagoil Bay. In practice the four Maids, and especially the *Argyll, Cumbrae*, and *Skelmorlie*, often exchanged duties on the Firth.

Left: Maid of Cumbrae dressed overall at Rothesay Pier. She is seen here in 1970 or 1971, with a black hull and lions on the funnels.

Below: Maid of Cumbrae, on the same occasion, seen from a steamer approaching the pier.

Bottom: In the winter of 1971-1972 *Maid of Cumbrae* was converted to a car ferry for the Gourock to Dunoon service. Her stern was cut away and a U-shaped covered car deck with a turntable at the apex was created forward on the main deck.

In 1973, after only one season as a car ferry with a yellow and black CSP funnel, *Maid of Cumbrae* swapped that for the red, yellow and black CalMac funnel, and is seen here in that condition at Dunoon Pier.

Above: Maid of Cumbrae was withdrawn in 1977 and sold. She left the Clyde under the name *Hanseatic*, but entered service in 1979 named *Noce di Cocco*, for Navigazione Alto Adriatico on a local service between Trieste and Muggia. (*Giorgio Spazzapan*)

Right: After less than a year at Trieste, the former Maid was sold to Neapolitan owners, and entered service in the Bay of Naples. In 1983, now named *Capri Express*, she was offering day cruises from Capri, complete with an inflatable swimming pool on the car deck. The covered portion of the car deck had been turned into a passenger lounge. At that time she still carried her lions on the funnel.

Above left: The day cruises were not a success and from 1984 *Capri Express* settled down to a regular existence on a Naples to Sorrento summer-only car ferry service. She is seen here leaving Naples Molo Beverello. At this time her hull was painted blue.

Capri Express, now with a white hull, departing Naples on 31 July 1998. (*Admeto Verde*)

139

In autumn 2000, *Capri Express* moved to the north of the Bay of Naples, chartered to the firm of Di Maio for the service from Pozzuoli to Procida, where, a few months later, she was joined by her sister *Ala*, ex-*Maid of Skelmorlie*, in year-round service. She is seen here at Procida on 23 September 2000. (*Arturo Lauriano, courtesy of Admeto Verde*)

Arran at Rothesay in the mid-sixties with *Waverley* astern of her. She entered service on 4 January 1954 on the Gourock to Dunoon service and later alternated with the other two car ferries in her class on that and the Wemyss Bay to Rothesay service and, until the arrival of *Glen Sannox* in 1957, the Ardrossan and Fairlie to Arran service. A thrice-weekly cargo service from Wemyss Bay to Millport was also offered.

Left: The other novelties of the 1953-1954 period were the ABC car ferries. They utilized hoist-loading, which was unique at that time on the Clyde, in British waters and probably worldwide. The method utilized existing piers without the necessity for expensive link-spans, but it had the disadvantage of being extremely slow, because after every six cars, or less, the hoist had to be lowered to the garage deck level, the cars driven off, and the hoist raised again. The first of these car ferries to enter service was *Arran*. Denny of Dumbarton launched her on 22 September 1953. Initially, as seen here, all three had king posts aft with derricks to load cargo and passenger's luggage to a small cargo deck aft of the lift. After about five years, these were removed and the section aft of the lift used as extra car-carrying space.

In 1970 *Arran* was transferred to David MacBrayne Ltd and used on the service from West Loch Tarbert, seen here, to Gigha, Islay, and Jura.

In early 1974 *Arran* was converted to a stern-loading car ferry at Barclay Curle's yard and, later that year, replaced by *Pioneer* on the Islay service, she returned to the Clyde, and is seen here at Kilreggan. At that time she had an additional starboard side ramp added for disembarking cars at Dunoon and Rothesay. The second Dunoon car ferry operated some contract runs to Kilreggan for workers engaged in the construction of the large submarine base at Coulport.

Arran leaving Gourock in spring 1979 with *Kenilworth*, the regular Kilcreggan ferry of Clyde Marine Motoring, at her berth in the foreground.

Arran was withdrawn in July 1979 and lay in Greenock's East India Harbour until she left under tow for Dublin in September 1981. As seen in this illustration, she was used there as a floating nightclub in the River Liffey (owned by the television celebrity Eamonn Andrews) and was built up aft over the former car deck, with a helicopter pad atop the new superstructure. In December 1986 she was moved to Salford Quays, Manchester, and renamed *Resolution* for a similar venture, but that did not transpire and she was broken up there in 1993.

Cowal was the second of the ABC class to be launched. She was launched on 20 January 1954 from the Ailsa yard at Troon and is seen her in a trials photograph.

Cowal prior to 1959 at Dunoon with *Bute* or *Arran* arriving from Gourock.

Cowal in a postcard view at Whiting Bay Pier in Arran, taken prior to 1959.

In 1970 *Cowal* was placed on a new service from Fairlie to Tarbert via Brodick, as a partial replacement for the now withdrawn MacBrayne mail service, and is seen here from *Maid of Argyll*, which was arriving on an excursion run from Gourock. This car ferry service only lasted for two summers, and was replaced by the crossing from Lochranza to Claonaig with *Kilbrannan* in 1972.

Top: This produced an unusual instance of double berthing on the Clyde, with *Maid of Argyll* alongside *Cowal* at Tarbert.

Middle: Cowal continued on the Wemyss Bay to Rothesay service, with occasional calls at the oil rig construction yard at Ardyne until withdrawn in 1977. In 1979 she was sold to Phetouris Ferries of Greece and left under tow for Perama. She is seen here in July 1981, partially rebuilt, still with the name *Cowal*. She was to have been named *Med Star*, and a service was advertised across the south of the Adriatic from Otranto to Igoumenitsa, but work was never completed, reportedly because of the death of the project leader. She was scrapped in 1984. (*Antonio Scrimali*)

Bottom: Bute was launched on 28 September 1954, also at Troon, and entered service in December of that year on the Wemyss Bay to Rothesay service. She is seen here on trials.

Cars being loaded on an unidentified ABC car ferry at Gourock. Note the diesel-electric paddle vessel *Talisman* berthed at the wires near the present car ferry ramp.

Bute arriving at Dunoon in the mid-sixties.

Bute at Largs in the mid-seventies, disembarking a caravan from Millport.

In 1979 the horns of the lift gear of *Bute* were extended to enable *Bute* to be used on the Mallaig to Armadale run. She was at that time the annual relief to *Loch Arkaig* on the Small Isles run and is seen here at Canna in this capacity. She also saw some service from Oban to Craignure in the early 1970s.

Top: *Bute* was also sold to Phetouris Ferries, and sailed for Piraeus on 17 June 1980. She was renamed *Med Sun*, but no work was done on her after arrival in Greece and she was broken up in 1985.

Middle: Only a few months after the entry of service of *Bute*, the announcement was made in April 1955 of a new larger car ferry of similar design for the Arran service. *Glen Sannox* was launched at the Ailsa yard at Troon on 30 April 1957 and entered service on 29 June of that year. As built she had a crane aft of the lift, and is seen here on trials.

Bottom: *Glen Sannox* at Gourock, with flags flying, on her delivery to the CSP.

149

Glen Sannox arriving at Fairlie at Easter 1964. During this period the winter sailings were maintained from Fairlie and in summer the Arran ferry berthed at Fairlie overnight. In 1964 she was the first member of the fleet to receive the lions on her funnel, and in 1965, the first to be painted in the blue hull.

Glen Sannox departing Brodick dressed overall on 18 May 1968, on the occasion of a Clyde River Steamer Club cruise round Arran. After Whiting Bay Pier was closed in 1962, Brodick was the only Arran Pier served by the car ferries.

Top: In the 1970-1971 winter the crane and aft superstructure was removed and *Glen Sannox* was converted to a stern-loading car ferry for the Gourock to Dunoon and, later, the Wemyss Bay to Rothesay services. She is seen here leaving Gourock.

Middle: Glen Sannox at a section of Gourock pier which is no longer in in existence in early 1976. In early 1977 she was refitted and re-engined at Hall Russell's yard at Aberdeen.

Bottom: In 1977, following the withdrawal of *Queen Mary, Glen Sannox* became CalMac's excursion vessel. Tables with umbrellas and plastic chairs appeared on the car deck, mobile stairs were provided from the promenade deck and white lines were painted round her hull. In 1978 and 1979 she provided sailings from Glasgow, but poor marketing and the success of *Waverley* proved to be too much. She is seen here at Wemyss Bay in that condition.

Glen Sannox at Rothesay in cruising condition. The tops of the sun umbrellas and the aircraft-step type mobile stairs can be seen.

In the winter months, *Glen Sannox* was used on the Oban to Craignure service, and is seen here in April 1980 at Oban from *Columba*, which had made a positioning voyage from the Clyde after refit, with a party of enthusiasts on board.

In 1989 *Glen Sannox* was sold to Greek owners and renamed *Nadia* and then *Knooz*. She is seen here in dry dock at Perama undergoing a rebuild with a new wheelhouse, having been fitted and undergoing work in building a new superstructure on her stern. She bore the names *Al Marwah* and later *Al Basmalah I*, operating in the Red Sea pilgrim trade, but was laid up for a long while and is believed to have been scrapped in summer 2000.

In 1967 a new motor vessel for the Largs to Millport (Old Pier) service was transferred from the Thames ferry service between Tilbury and Gravesend. *Rose* was one of a trio built in 1961 by J.S. White at Cowes. She entered service on 12 June 1967 and, after running for a couple of weeks with the name *Rose*, she was renamed *Keppel*. She is seen here in July 1968 from Keppel Pier.

Top: Keppel on 22 August 1970, passing *Queen Mary II* which is just leaving Keppel Pier, and about to be passed by the hovercraft *HM2-011*. *(Andrew Clark)*

Above: Keppel in 1975 at Largs Pier with *Queen Mary II*.

Left: Early in her Clyde career, *Keppel* received a larger funnel, rather than the funnel-cum-mast that she had originally carried. Her Largs to Millport service was withdrawn in May 1986 and she became the Clyde cruise vessel, mainly serving piers in the nearer parts of the firth because of her lack of speed. These included Tighnabruiach and Carrick Castle, the first time a CSP Vessel had made regular calls there since the 1930s.

In 1993, *Keppel* was withdrawn, sold to a Greenock operator and renamed *Clyde Rose*, although the new name was never registered as such. She was repainted with a blue funnel, and was intended to operate charters, although few actually took place. At the end of that season she was laid up and eventually sold to Malta, where she operates round-the-island excursions under the name of *Keppel*.

In August 1969 the CSP, now under the aegis of the Scottish Transport Group, purchased Arran Piers Ltd from the family of the late Duke and Duchess of Hamilton. This enabled them to install a link-span at Brodick to enable the use of a drive-through car ferry, and *Stena Baltica* was purchased from the Swedish operator, Stena Line, for this purpose. She had been built in 1966 at Langesund in Norway for their route from Gothenburg to Frederikshavn, and later operated on 'The Londoner' service from Tilbury to Calais. She is seen here at Calais in a postcard view, with SNCF's *Compiegne* behind her and Sealink's *Invicta* in the background.

Top: Stena Baltica in the Garvel dry dock at Greenock in April 1970, refitting prior to entering service on the Clyde. By this time she had been re-registered at Glasgow, but still carried her Stena name.

Middle: Stena Baltica was renamed *Caledonia* and is seen here at the roll-on roll-off facility provided by Clydeport at Ardrossan. She entered service on the Ardrossan to Brodick sailing on 29 May 1970. By now, all sailings were from Ardrossan and Fairlie Pier was no longer used.

Bottom: Caledonia arriving at Brodick in a postcard view. The new causeway leading out to the link-span can be seen in this illustration.

In 1974, *Caledonia* was moved to the Oban to Craignure service in summer, although remaining on the Arran route in winter, and is seen here in a postcard view at Oban.

Caledonia departing Brodick at Easter 1984, with *Waverley* arriving and *Glen Sannox* in the distance.

Top: At the end of the 1987 season, *Caledonia* was withdrawn, being now too small for the traffic on offer. She was purchased by a buyer on the East Coast of Scotland, and was taken to Dundee for proposed use as a floating restaurant, but this never occurred and about a year later she was sold to Bay of Naples purchasers Linee Lauro, where she entered service between Pozzuoli and Ischia as *Heidi. (R. Starcevich)*

Middle: Heidi continues to operate on this crossing, now under the green and yellow colours of Traghetti Pozzuoli. *(Arturo Lauriano, courtesy of Admeto Verde)*

Bottom: HM2-011 departing from Largs. She only lasted for two seasons on the Clyde, and was then returned to her builders.

In 1970 the CSP introduced a Hovermarine HM-2 hovercraft, *HM2-011*. She operated from Gourock to Dunoon, Rothesay, Largs and Millport, and is seen here at the latter location in summer 1970.

In 1972, a new car ferry service from Largs to Cumbrae Slip, near the former Tattie Pier on Cumbrae, was commenced. This was operated by two former Kyle to Kyleakin ferries, *Largs*, ex-*Kyleakin* of 1960, and *Coruisk* of 1969. Both were withdrawn in 1986. *Largs* is seen here arriving at Largs.

In 1972, the last vessel to wear the buff black-topped CSP funnel entered service, *Kilbrannan*, was the first of what would be a series of eight Island-class ferries built by James Lamont & Co. Ltd at Port Glasgow. She inaugurated a new service from Lochranza to Claonaig at the top of the Kintyre peninsula on 8 July 1972. These small ferries were affectionately known to steamer enthusiasts as the 'Daft Ducks'.

The last vessel for which the Caledonian Steam Packet signed a contract was the Gourock to Dunoon ferry *Jupiter*, although she did not enter service until 1974. She continues in service to the present day on the Gourock to Dunoon and Wemyss Bay to Rothesay routes. For many years she carried a metal CSP pennant on her jack staff forward, and her lions are those formerly carried by *Maid of Skelmorlie*, transferred on the sale of the Maid.